JUMP START

Ideas to Move Your Mind

Beatrice J. Elyé
with Catherine A. Southwick

Gifted Psychology Press, Inc.
P.O. Box 5057
Scottsdale, AZ 85261
www.giftedbooks.com

SALVE REGINA UNIVERSITY

JumpStart: Ideas to Move Your Mind

Cover Design: ATG Productions, Inc.
Interior Design: Spring Winnette

Published by
Gifted Psychology Press, Inc.
P.O. Box 5057
Scottsdale, AZ 85261
www.giftedbooks.com

Printed and Bound in the United States of America

04 03 02 01 5 4 3 2 1

Library of Congress Cataloging-in-Publication Data

Elyé, Beatrice J. (Beatrice Josephine), 1928-
    Jumpstart: ideas to move your mind / Beatrice J. Elyé with Catherine A. Southwick.
        p. cm.
    Includes bibliographical references and indexes.
    ISBN 0-910707-40-5
    1. Teenagers--Life skills guides. [1. Life skills.] I. Southwick, Catherine A. (Catherine
Ann), 1969-II. Title.

HQ796.E567 2001
646.7'00835--dc21   00-062293

ISBN 0-910707-40-5

Dedication

This book is dedicated to my first and best teachers—my parents; to all the students I had the privilege of teaching; to my encouraging friends; and to many wonderful librarians.

Acknowledgements

Writing *JumpStart* would have been an insurmountable challenge without the help of Catherine Ann Southwick. In our many discussions concerning its content, we established wonderful rapport and often spent hours evaluating the appropriateness of a single word. Both of us hunted for quotations that would amplify and extend the meaning of the ideas in each chapter. She provided a contemporary viewpoint that made the selection process of these quotations a challenge. I hereby acknowledge her capable determination, valuable insights, and intellectual integrity; without her help, this book might never have been published.

Another friend and esteemed colleague, Carol Hibbard, critically reviewed each of the original chapters. With her wisdom and language skills, she spent many hours perusing both the original papers upon which this book is based and some of the final rewritten chapters. Her careful and intelligent critique resulted in changes that have made the reading easier and more informative.

I am grateful to Dr. James T. Webb and the editors at Gifted Psychology Press, Inc. for their invaluable help in preparing this book for publication.

Finally, I owe major gratitude to a large number of those creative people who informed my life with their wit and insight. Their creative expressions expanded my knowledge of the human condition. They have given me alternative ideas, and showed me by their choices that living is a selective process where decisions may be influenced by cultural and societal experiences. I especially admire people who fulfill their promise despite handicaps or difficult circumstances. One of my heroes is Nelson Mandela; therefore, it seems appropriate to quote a selection from his 1994 inaugural speech. These powerful words describe his sense of what thoughtful people must do. His words also suggest how and why I will be thankful if this book has meaning for you.

> *Our deepest fear is not that we are inadequate. Our deepest fear is that we are powerful beyond measure. It is our light, not our darkness that most frightens us.*
>
> *We ask ourselves, "Who am I to be brilliant, gorgeous, talented, and fabulous?" Actually, who are you not to be? Your playing small does not serve the world. There's nothing enlightened about shrinking so that other people won't feel insecure around you.*
>
> *As we let our own light shine, we unconsciously give other people permission to do the same.*
>
> **– Nelson Mandela**

Table of Contents

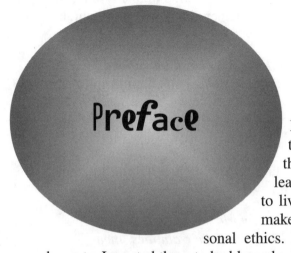

Preface

I had dreams for every kid I taught. I wanted each of them to be happy, to enjoy learning enough to ache for it, to live an examined life, and to make decisions based upon personal ethics. I hoped they would prize honesty. I wanted them to be blessed with good friends and to treasure family. In retrospect, I realize that I did not care if they became "successes" in the competitive modern sense of that term, but I always expected them to do their best at whatever they did.

For their sake, and that of future generations, I wanted them to appreciate both the beauty of the earth as well as its fragility, especially as an environment for all forms of life. I tried to share with them what I treasure—the ability to reason and the desire to delight in the amazing insights provided by scientists, writers, artists, and musicians, among others. I wanted them to learn that every experiment is a personal trip into the unknown, with guidelines of observation and analysis of data as their only compass. Furthermore, I wanted them to understand that experimentation is the fundamental basis of each person's life journey; every day contains new adventures and experiments that shape us.

I believe that everyone has talent. I also believe that all of us must use whatever mental abilities we possess, wisely and without arrogance. Just as we benefit daily from the efforts of all of those who have preceded us—using their discoveries and enjoying their creative works—so are we obliged to provide future generations with the fruits of our creative efforts.

Using and developing one's abilities should not simply be drudgery, however. To me, there is a joy within the search process that accompanies creative effort—a pleasure that I tried to impart to my students. The following quote from Mark Twain's *Life on the Mississippi* represents, in a poetic manner, this sense of pleasurable creativity.

> *When I am playful, I use the meridians of longitude and parallels of latitude for a seine, and drag the Atlantic Ocean for whales. I scratch my head with the lightning and purr myself to sleep with the thunder.*

I also believe it is important to know oneself. The journalist Sydney J. Harris sums it up this way:

> *Ninety percent of the world's woe comes from people not knowing themselves, their abilities, their frailties, and even their real virtues. Most of us go almost all the way through life as complete strangers to ourselves—so how can we know anyone else?*

You may have wonderful dreams that can be realized by using some of the suggestions in this book. I hope that JumpStart will be a book that you will write in, and thus personalize and expand it with your own ideas as you read the various chapters. Blank pages have been inserted in each chapter exactly for that purpose. At some future time you may enjoy rereading sections, especially because your comments may trigger new thoughts and changes in direction. They may give you a sense of who you were, who you are now, and how you have grown. Upon rereading, you may say to yourself, "Did I really write this or think that?" And on the journey of life—that adventure with so few signposts—perhaps you will come to better know yourself.

This book is a collection of insights culled from my own experiments in living. I enjoy being creative and developed various skills both by joining scholarly pursuits and by seeking innovative activities. Some of the events in my life could have been overwhelming if I had used less thoughtful methods of reacting to problems. Instead, I not only found ways to take pleasure in what was possible, but also often managed to convert the possible into improbable good fortune. My life has been a marvelous adventure. I hope you will find some of my ideas useful to your adventuring. I wish you the best of journeys.

Postscript: In writing JumpStart, *I chose not to use the words I, me, and mine. Even so, I hope you will consider the book to be a conversation between us, with me being the obviously talkative one. And like all talk, some parts will be more interesting to you than others. Save those parts for another day, when they may be suddenly more useful.*

How To Use This Book

This book is based on material that I used as a teacher of high school students, ages 14–18, who were doing well in school, either achieving high grades or obviously possessing special talents. These students were full of idealism and dreams for the world and their futures, but often lacked experience and skills in areas like time management, decision making, organization of meetings, and group skills that would make them effective leaders. I realized that a book of ideas, based on my experiences, could help other high school and college students, as well as many adults, to improve their mental, creative, and self-management skills.

I suggest reading each chapter at a pace that allows you to complete the recommended exercises or activities before proceeding to the next chapter. You do not need to read the chapters in sequence. Instead, you can choose chapters based on your personal need or a chapter's appeal. Although many books assume that one chapter builds on preceding ones, this book does not. Exceptions are the first chapter, titled **Personal Notebooks**, which is referred to throughout the book, and the last chapter, **All of Your Tomorrows**, which contains references to previous chapters. You may want to scan the Table of Contents as well as the summary near the end of each chapter in order to locate desirable material for you.

Blank pages between chapters are for your notes, personal reactions, comments, creative writings, or perhaps sketches. This will be a convenient way for you to keep them for future reference.

I have selected topics for each chapter based on their importance to a creative life. Some of the chapters may help you with practical

xiv JUMPSTART **Ideas to Move Your Mind**

activities, such as speed reading. Other chapters provide useful information on managing personal problems, such as frustration. Still other chapters discuss thought processes, such as decision making.

I have highlighted ideas, people, and events about which you may wish to gather more information by inserting the symbol 📖. Words that you may wish to look up to better understand their context are followed by the symbol ✍.

Whether you are using this book for yourself, or whether you are using it to mentor others, the following suggestions may help you get the most out of *JumpStart*:

1. Quickly scan the chapter to locate citations containing the 📖 symbol, and gather any materials or references you will need to research them. Doing research outside of your normal range of interests will help you extend your knowledge. For example, with the chapter on Personal Notebooks you might do the following:

   - Inspect various kinds and sizes of notebooks, and select a favorite to use.
   - Locate a good dictionary in which to look up words followed by the ✍ symbol.
   - Listen to one or more of the three cited musical compositions.
   - Locate reference materials on Leonardo da Vinci and Charles Darwin.
   - Find a reproduction of Picasso's *Guernica*; locate information on the Spanish Civil War.
   - Find some of Anton Chekhov's writing—perhaps his play *The Cherry Orchard*.
   - Set up a display of common household discards that are not normally recycled.
   - Collect and scan various newspapers—local, out-of-town, national, and foreign.

2. Reread the chapter more slowly this time. Use the reference materials you have collected to assist in understanding the

concepts. Develop any ideas suggested by the chapter.

3. Attend events at local cultural institutions as suitable sources of inspiration and/or rewards for your hard work.

4. Refer to other chapters as you proceed, especially those having continuing applications, such as **Creative Thought Processes** and **The Time of Your Life**.

5. If you are mentoring an individual or a group, discuss each chapter and share reactions *on a voluntary basis*.

6. Use *JumpStart* over an extended period of time. Each chapter could "stir the mind" initially for as much as one to two weeks, including time to complete, reflect, and assimilate.

7. Consider how you can use your new insights to further your goals and dreams. I truly hope that *JumpStart: Ideas to Move Your Mind* will do exactly as its title suggests.

8. Three aids are provided to help you search for information now and in the future. Use the brief summary near the end of each chapter to locate general content. The first index at the end of the book lists the names of people mentioned in the text, including authors of cited books. The second index lists authors and the first three words of their quotes as they appear throughout this book. However, the best index may be the one you can create for yourself. Such an index could be derived from specific content you highlight or note in the margins. Also, it could include items from a personal action agenda of things you want to do, responses on the "Your Ideas" pages, concepts that need additional exploration, and reflections upon reading any of the books in the bibliographies.

Finally, you are entitled to know something about my philosophy and beliefs. The core of what I consider important, relative to this book, is the following:

- Life is a journey of self-discovery, a learning experience. Honesty is the mirror I must use to search my innermost being. A quote from Shakespeare's *Hamlet* says it well. "This above all. To thine own self be true,

And it must follow, as the night the day, thou canst not then be false to any man."

- My life depends on how I manage it daily—moment by moment. No one else should be held accountable more than I for any part of my life (assuming that I am able to think and am in reasonable health). I am not suggesting that I have complete freedom; no one does. But I can respond sensibly to challenges, problems, and opportunities, even when I do not have control of a situation. I may need to be inventive, and there will be occasions when I am overwhelmed; then I must accept help.

- I am not able to change until I am ready to be influenced. In almost all human interaction, the readiness factor is the basis of meaningful change. For example, learning is a shared responsibility, a contract between student and teacher.

- Life should be joyous and have many moments of happiness. Bubbles of laughter are yeast for my creativity, a satisfying part of my life. I must actively pursue happiness.

- I must treasure life. This means being thoughtful in all human interactions, being kind to all life, and respecting that which supports life, the environment. When I fail, as I will on occasion, I must seek to correct my mistakes.

The items in my list are not ranked in any particular order—all are equally important; any one may predominate in a particular situation. Perhaps your own set of beliefs will become clearer to you as you read this book.

Chapter 1
Personal Notebooks

Throughout history, many famous and creative people have kept notebooks to record their reflections and experiences, among them Leonardo da Vinci 📖 and Charles Darwin 📖.

You don't need to be famous, however, to find keeping a notebook helpful. I believe you will find it invaluable in improving your observational and creative thinking skills.

Your choice for a notebook depends upon your plan for using it. Small, pocket size notebooks are ideal for being constant companions. Larger ones provide more space for writing and can be kept in some convenient special place such as bedside, desk, or locker. Ruled paper, art sketchbooks, or bound blank paper books—all have various advantages and are commercially available.

The most important part of your notebook is not its form, but rather its content. Your purpose in journaling should be to record ideas. That is, this journal is not the diary-type to record what you did when or where, nor is it the classroom information-type, useful for fact retrieval. Instead, it is primarily for your personal observations, thoughts, and concepts.

Try the following. Think of something that you are interested in—a problem, something that you wish to make or do, or something that you hope to understand. Think about it in your spare moments, *persistently* &⌢. Consider or fantasize all kinds of possibilities; then write them in your notebook. Actually "picture" solutions to the problem. Wherever you are, look at some object and try to find a relationship to your idea or problem. Your ideas may seem wild, silly, or even apparently hopeless, but record them anyway. Would radio or television have made sense in the 1800s? Let your mind freely explore, and describe your thoughts in your notebook.

This process of describing, which allows you to focus on your creative idea, could be verbal, pictorial, or musical. Let your descriptions be both expansive and passionate. The *Grand Canyon Suite* 📖, *Mood Indigo* 📖, and *Ebbtide* 📖 are each musical descriptions. Picasso's *Guernica* 📖 is a powerful pictorial description of his reaction to the bombing of the Basque capital in the Spanish Civil War and exemplifies that ideas provide the seed for actions that come much later. Ideas alone did not create Picasso's painting, but ideas had to precede its creation. Eventually Picasso acted upon his political beliefs by creating this masterpiece to depict the agony of war.

Ideas recorded in your notebook—however sketchy, brief, or tentative—can be the initial stage of eventually finding something worth transforming into concrete form. Of course, you may not use any of your early ideas, but the practice of writing and describing your concepts is a useful exercise to make your future efforts at creativity easier and more valuable to you and others. Remember, at this point you need not be concerned with the practicality of your entries. Techniques for evaluating ideas are suggested in other chapters of this book (see Chapters 3, 4, and 7).

Your notebook may be used for a variety of purposes. It is to be your treasure trove &⌢ of any appealing tidbit that can be creatively rearranged or thought about in a new context. You may wish to note ideas or actions that seem to be innovative and useful. For example, you might imagine how some household items could be recycled into usable objects. Perhaps you might diagram or describe these objects in your notebook.

You could set aside a part of your notebook to record unusual information that appeals to you, such as a famous quotation, news events, bits of conversation, descriptions, unusual words, or terms. Many authors maintain records of chance conversations overheard in public places because they like the phrasing or wish to make sure they remember the concepts.

You could also set aside a portion of your notebook for poetry and other metaphorical ᘓᐤwriting. Writing poetry is a great mind-sharpener. You might find Anton Chekhov's 📖 advice to his brother worthwhile: "In descriptions one must seize upon small details, grouping them so that when the reader closes his eyes, he gets a picture. For instance, you'll have a moonlit night if you write that on the mill dam a piece of glass from a broken bottle glittered like a bright star." You could write a daily aphorism ᘓᐤ. Aim at making it personal, imaginative, and perhaps quotable.

Other notebook entries could include a description of something, perhaps written from an imagined viewpoint other than your own. How would a thinking worm describe daily events seen along the edge of a pond? This requires "double think"—not just what you would sense, but what someone or something else would sense.

Whether or not you are artistic, attempt to sketch something from your surroundings. Do this on a regular basis to sharpen observation skills.

From the newspaper, select and focus on an issue that interests you. Social, political, scientific, and artistic problems abound. Imagine that you are in a position to work on that problem. Use your notebook to brainstorm ᘓᐤ your ideas and to summarize whatever relevant information is available. Record your opinions regarding this problem. Talk to people about these issues. Perhaps you may wish to write letters to persons who are in a position to influence the problem, and include these letters in your notebook.

Remember to date each notebook entry to provide both a sense of history and perspective. If you think you have an exceptionally good idea, have your record notarized. (Many banks and real estate offices have personnel who can notarize material for little or no cost.) This would be valuable in case you later wish to make a patent ᘓᐤ or copyright application. For this reason, make sure that this notebook is bound in such a way that pages cannot be inserted or removed unless binding or paging is affected.

Above all, remember that your personal notebooks are very special. They are meant to be a source of fun and excitement, not a chore. Ten years from now they will likely still delight you, and may even serve as a source of additional ideas.

Summary

☞ Keep a personal notebook.

☞ Use it to record any ideas that interest you.

☞ Include in your notebook creative responses to ideas.

☞ Reexamine its content occasionally.

Words
of
Wisdom

I do not think that I will ever reach a stage when I will say, "That is what I believe. Finished." What I believe is alive ... and open to growth ... .
–Madeleine L'Engle

I think that one's art is a growth inside one. I do not think one can explain growth. It is silent and subtle. One does not keep digging up a plant to see how it grows.
–Emily Carr

Bring ideas in and entertain them royally, for one of them may be the king.
–Mark Van Doren

Man's mind stretched to a new idea never goes back to its original dimensions.
–Oliver Wendell Holmes

Ideas should be received like guests—in a friendly way, but with the reservation that they are not to tyrannize their host.
–Alberto Moravia

Use what language you will, you can never say anything but what you are.
–Ralph Waldo Emerson

Your Ideas

The great art of writing is the art of making people real to themselves with words.   **–Logan Pearsall Smith**

Your Ideas

_____

_____

_____

_____

_____

_____

_____

_____

_____

_____

_____

_____

_____

_____

_____

_____

_____

_____

_____

_____

The events in our lives happen in a sequence in time but in their significance to ourselves they find their own order ... the continuous thread of revelation.
                                                    –Eudora Welty

Chapter 2
The Time
of Your Life

Very busy people seem to accomplish more than others do. In fact, a common expression is, "If you want something done, ask a busy person." Why? Because busy people are often more efficient users of their time and can be counted on to get the job done. Everyone has 24 hours in a day, but nearly all of us can learn to use this limited resource more efficiently. Often we squander ᴖ time. Yet, as Benjamin Franklin said, "Lost time is never found again." The time we waste because we have not planned its best uses is the most costly expenditure of our lives.

To better manage your time, first list your daily and weekly activities to help you discover how you currently use your time. Most people have an average of at least four hours of "discretionary" time (D-Time) per day, sometimes called "leisure" time. This is time *not* required for work, school, or family-related obligations, or for health maintenance. In your notebook, prepare a personal chart of the D-Time you anticipate you will have for a period of at least a week, noting half-hour intervals. After the week, examine the data. Are you satisfied with your time usage? If not, what would you like to change?

Consider what you really wish to accomplish—this week, this month, this year. Some people's lives are like wasted arrows. They go fast and far, but not where the archer intended. By contrast, some people focus their energies and abilities in such a way as to achieve as much as possible. Sometimes people feel a sense of obligation to leave something behind for posterity—for the preservation of humanity, civilization, and their heirs. For some people, this may represent a search for fame, or they may consider their efforts a form of "repayment" for the bounteous ✍ gifts of predecessors ✍. For others, simply the joy derived from creative efforts becomes an incentive.

What motivates you? How do you want to live?

As a suggestion, carefully think right now about your future, your innermost desires, and your talents and abilities. Then, list in your personal notebook—or on the blank pages at the end of this chapter—no more than three accomplishments that you would like to achieve this year.

Is the time management in your present D-Time chart likely to help you achieve those goals? If not, what changes could you effect? The following suggestions may help:

1. Obtain or make a calendar that has space for you to write daily entries. Within D-Time periods, make notations or appointments for activities that you think might help you reach your goals. For example, set aside Monday from 4 to 6 p.m. to research colleges known to be strong in mathematics (or some other subject that interests you). Consider this appointment with yourself to be as important as a doctor's appointment. Regular use of such a calendar to record daily activities is one of the best ways to organize your time.

2. Make lists of ideas related to your goals. Suppose that you want to do more reading and creative writing. Your list might look something like this:

• Go to the main library once each month and the local branch library weekly, and check out two new books each visit.

- Go to local bookstores, set up a book-buying budget, and begin building a personal library.
- Set up a card file of titles, authors, or topics that you want to read (or read more about).
- Use information from the Internet when possible, and establish computer files about topics you are interested in.
- Regularly read the *New York Times Book Review Section* or other book reviews.
- Write a poem, essay, or portion of a short story each week, and send letters of inquiry to publishers asking how your writing might become published.

When
- Work for one hour every morning and for two hours on Saturday or Sunday.
- List your schedule of activities on your calendar or in your notebook.

3. If your D-time for desired activities is hampered by other obligations, be creative. Get up earlier, swap chores with a sibling, or seek ways to save time spent on routine activities. Aim at having better control of all your time. You may discover that some of your activities are unnecessary, but have become habitual ∽.

4. Plan each week separately, listing the entire month's activities, including D-time, to the extent known.

5. Schedule recreation and rewards. For example, as soon as the outline of your Chapter 1 is completed, use part of the next weekend for a holiday.

6. Ask yourself, "Does this contribute something essential or desirable to my life or that of others?" This question will weed out overly frivolous ∽ use of your time.

7. Get enough rest. You will be happier and more productive.

Summary

☞ Prepare a personal time chart, including D-time.

☞ Study your time usage for possible improvement.

☞ List a few desired accomplishments for this year, and set aside time to work on them.

☞ Make and use a large appointment-type calendar to schedule your times.

☞ Make a list of long-term goals.

☞ Carefully examine daily routines.

☞ Schedule rewards.

☞ Regularly "question" your use of time.

What I do today is important because I am exchanging a day of my life for it.
–Hugh Mulligan

It's not what you were, it's what you are today.
–David Marion

The opportunity of life is very precious and it moves very quickly.
–Ilyani Ywahoo

There is no such thing in anyone's life as an unimportant day.
–Alexander Woollcott

Ultimately, time is all you have and the idea isn't to save it but to savor it.
–Ellen Goodman

Time is the coin of your life. It is the only coin you have, and only you can determine how it will be spent. Be careful lest you let other people spend it for you.
–Carl Sandburg

Your Ideas

Time flies over us, but leaves its shadow behind.
–Nathaniel Hawthorne

Your Ideas

_____

_____

_____

_____

_____

_____

_____

_____

_____

_____

_____

_____

_____

_____

_____

_____

_____

_____

_____

_____

_____

Each day, and the living of it, has to be a conscious creation in which discipline and order are relieved with some play and pure foolishness.
– May Sarton

Chapter 3
Observation

How do you know what you know? Is there a common source for all knowledge? The following scenarios may help you develop an answer to these questions. Think about how each scenario differs from the others and what they have in common.

Scenario 1

Unexpectedly, your team has just won a championship. Sweat is pouring down your face. The roar from the crowd chips away your teammates' words as you joyously high five and hug one another. You look toward the bleachers and see faces with incredible clarity. Every part of you is achingly alive.

Scenario 2

Everyone has been blindfolded in an experiment on sensitivity. Your first task is to determine your position in the room. Physical chaos occurs as people bump into furniture and each other. But by standing still and listening, you hope to find your way to your own chair. It is not an easy activity.

Scenario 3 You gaze into a deep valley overhung with grey clouds spitting tongues of gold. Surrounding you are fields of asters, a scent of sweetness, and the low grumbling sounds of thunder. You snatch a single flower stalk and sweep it around your head with whoops of joy. Then you quickly gather your belongings, including the best water color painting you have ever made, and run for cover before the rain starts.

What did all of these descriptions have in common? Each scene described sensory responses to the environment. Major events, because they are dangerous, exciting, and/or totally engrossing ᐭ, can increase your sensitivity to your surroundings (Scenario 1). Your observational skills are subconscious and sometimes not acknowledged until they are threatened or changed (Scenario 2). When your senses are stimulated by interesting, beautiful, or unique circumstances, your observations and responses can be extraordinary (Scenario 3).

As a baby, you probably observed that crying brought you attention, and you learned to time your efforts accordingly. When you wanted someone to pick you up, you were willing to expend the energy to cry. Successes reinforced these efforts, and part of your personality may have been forged by those early wails. You learned to observe cause and effect, and these early experiences contributed both to your inventory of observations as well as your skill in observing.

Do you remember a time in childhood when a dandelion blossom was worth lengthy, intense observation? Or when you played with the same simple objects over and over again? That "play" was self-education—your personal discovery of the world. However, formal schooling interfered, to some extent, with your direct sensory experience. Opinions, descriptions, and values of others became substitutes. Perhaps the sensory pleasures of puffing at dandelion seed heads disappeared.

Your ability to observe and explore with a child's eye has diminished ᐭ. You seldom have the time for direct observation of the real thing. You make do with substitutes such as books, pictures, or models. A photograph, even with its problems of scale and incomplete sensory information, can become more real than the object or event represented. A television sequence becomes a "slice of life." But when you continuously work with second-hand information, your chances of really seeing, and really knowing, lessen. Second-hand information creates myriad *&* sensory data that are compressed into something—not the real thing, but better than nothing. Vicarious *&* sensing is a crutch that allows you to make-do. Superficially you know more, but the essence of reality is lost.

It is worthwhile to maintain your child's eye perspective which has few preconceived expectations or biases *&* and which is one of the most important sources of creativity. When events become commonplace, we take them for granted, and often the appreciation of their value diminishes. We recognize objects we handle daily, but without conscious recall of their detail. When you see something, what do you really see? How accurately? With what purpose? With what influence of previous experience? How much are you affected by cultural background, biological inheritance, and education in any particular observational situation?

Participating in an event such as mountain climbing produces information that is multi-dimensional; you are involving all of your senses. Your observations of such a direct experience are vividly emblazoned within your mind. You can build on this knowledge and memory with confidence. You have faith in its validity; you were there. You have obtained "active-sensory" or primary-source knowledge. Such personal experience of the world is preferable, but since it is difficult and time-consuming to directly acquire such sensory knowledge, using secondary sources is easier and a more practical way to expand what you know.

Reading or seeing pictures about mountain climbing also produces information—of the "passive-sensory" or secondary-source type. Before you can accept secondary-source knowledge in any new context, you need to be assured that it was obtained by capable people who observed reality directly themselves. Perhaps you have experienced an occasion when someone inaccurately observed one of your actions and thereby caused problems. Such misrepresentations frequently occur between people.

On a worldwide basis, observational errors exist in many areas of interpersonal relations, e.g., entrepreneurial ⤳, social, political, and diplomatic. Unintentional errors also occur in accepted knowledge sources such as books, journals, and the Internet. Purposeful errors are the basis of propaganda ⤳. In fact, erroneous and careless use of secondary-source material is perhaps the greatest modern threat to intelligent living. We live in an era ⤳ of information overload that makes information summaries appear enticing. This means that in situations where you must use summaries by others (i.e., secondary sources) you need to be vigilant, neither accepting nor rejecting ideas without careful thought.

Consider the following common statements:

1. "I need to see it for myself."
2. "If I am to be a leader, I need to talk directly to the people I will be leading."
3. "Only after I see the play do I read the reaction of the critics."
4. "I know what the experts say—but if they disagree, how can they be experts?"
5. "She is a teacher, so what she says must be right."

Examples 1, 2, and 3 refer to active sensory situations. Example 4 suggests a skeptical examination of secondary sources. Example 5 indicates a possible non-critical acceptance of a secondary source. As a thoughtful person, you will evaluate secondary source summaries for yourself.

Underlying all of your activities and everyday choices is the process of observation, either by you or by others. But it is one's critical examination of any observational process that results in creative insights. Observation—whether from primary or secondary sources—influences your decisions and beliefs, and thus indirectly determines what you can accomplish. Consider the politician who maintains direct contact with the people who elect him. He gathers evidence of their needs from conversations with his constituents ⤳.

Because of his frequent direct observations, he is more likely to sponsor practical legislation than another politician who has less direct contact with the people who elected him.

Observation serves a multitude of purposes, including the ability to identify, locate, and know. How do you know that a particular object belongs to you? What identifying clues do you use? If you had to claim a lost object, how accurately could you describe it? Ordinarily, such precision is unnecessary. For example, as you sit reading this, you are probably unaware of the weight of your shoes or clothes or wristwatch—at least you were, until now when your observation is focused on them. Much of what you sense throughout the day becomes static 〰, squelched by a properly functioning biological system. Without such selective awareness, observational overload would occur, and you would become fatigued by the vast number of sensory signals.

You tend to use your senses at varying levels of intensity, much like settings on a stove. The lowest "setting" is the subconscious, and then a few conscious impressions filter in, with more and more being recorded until a "red hot" alert takes place and extreme sensitivity occurs. This is why looking at something intensely can lead to an uncommon and particularly keen awareness. However, it is difficult to maintain such intense focus for a long time. Your mind may wander off target. Exercises in concentrated attention and "centering," which have been an important part of Eastern culture for centuries, can help maintain focus. Recently, some of these techniques have entered Western civilization via Zen 📖 publications and centers.

If you wish to explore Zen and its related areas, your public library or bookstore can be helpful. One particularly interesting book is *The Three Pillars of Zen* by Philip Kapleau. Another is *60 Seconds to Mind Expansion* by Harold Cook and Joel Davitz. The latter book describes brief exercises designed to increase sensory awareness. *New Mind, New Body, Bio-feedback: New Directions for the Mind* by Barbara B. Brown, Ph.D., provides information on the relationship of alpha brain waves to Zen and hypnosis, plus comments on parapsychology 📖, visual and auditory signals, mind-body music or art, and the medical usefulness of bio-feedback 📖.

What are some ways to improve your own sensory skills? The following list provides techniques and ideas. If you like, select some and use them frequently. You might like to use your personal notebook or the blank pages in this book to record your impressions, thoughts, and results.

Observe with Concentration

Make a focused effort to use all of your five senses while blotting out conscious thought as thoroughly as possible. Just look at something common—a key, a coin—for a brief period of time, and focus on what you see. *Listen* to household sounds with your eyes closed, and concentrate on what you hear. *Touch* objects and hold them so that you really feel their shape, weight, texture, etc. *Look* with fresh eyes at clouds, your bedroom blinds, or your hand. *Taste* food, a small mouthful at a time, feel the sensations, and try to identify ingredients. Check familiar objects for odors, or get a bouquet of flowers and *smell* each separate blossom, noting how each is unique. Sometimes you might want to consider the unusual properties of an object—the ones not quickly or easily noted. For example, in looking at a key you may focus on its shape, surface color, and reflectivity while also recording mentally a lack of obvious odor. Contrary thinking, examining, and observing the extraordinary in the seemingly ordinary can yield interesting ideas.

Observe Repeatedly

Examine the same objects over a period of time, possibly under different circumstances. Note how changes in you, emotional or mental, may affect your sensations, and how you begin to notice new aspects as time goes by. Seek a series of related events to observe for a prolonged period of time, perhaps months. People, weather, buildings, or a certain landscape, are possibilities. Record and keep these impressions if you wish.

Observe for a Purpose

As you collect observations, search for relationships within them. Make hypotheses 📖 about possible similarities, differences, cycles, patterns, and anomalies 📖. Set up a schedule of observations designed to confirm or deny the expected relationships. Be careful. People tend, often unconsciously, to try to confirm first impressions. So strong is this tendency that you may ignore contradictory evidence. Use blinds or controls 📖 in order to minimize the likelihood that you are only confirming your initial beliefs.

Observe to Trigger Your Imagination

Investigate something and then mentally play with its essential characteristics. Imagine what would be necessary for it to be something else. How could it be similar to something that superficially 📖 appears to be very different? For example, what are the differences between a car and an orange? How are they similar? Make your own pairings as ridiculous and extreme as possible. Then examine the objects and fantasize. Alternatively, look at something, observe it, and try to imagine what it is like at levels beyond your ability to sense. You can sense the size, texture, color, and odor of a sheet of paper. But what lies beyond what you can see, feel, or smell? What does the paper release that you cannot observe? What inner structure is concealed? What equipment could you use to improve your observation?

Observe with Feedback

Sketch something that you have observed, then compare your sketch with the actual object. You might use yourself, a pet, your room, your watch, etc. Some of these, such as your face, have emotional overtones that will affect your efforts considerably. The important thing here is not your artistic ability, but your abstraction of reality as you see it. If you cannot draw, describe the object without naming it.

Then ask someone to identify the object based solely on your written description

Observe Yourself

This may be challenging, difficult, and enjoyable. Ask yourself many questions, and then observe yourself. How long are your arms? How small an object can you see or feel? What sounds make you happy? How much food will you consume this week? How much peripheral ᴧ vision do you have? Are you perhaps clinically colorblind? In a room crowded with people, where would you choose to sit? How many words can you clearly speak in one minute? How far can you run in one minute? How accurately can you hear people speak? How much can you remember? What kinds of things do you remember? Can your fingertips distinguish between china and glass? These questions are just suggestions. Make up your own questions and find answers according to your interests.

Perhaps all of the emphasis on careful observation may seem like unnecessary effort to you. This chapter contains allusions ᴧ to the outcomes of observing a toy train and studying a baby's cry. Yet observations such as these, made under complex conditions, have led to important ideas. In the aforementioned book by Dr. Barbara Brown, a toy train was used to explore biofeedback. Results of her work may result in a decrease in premature deaths. Can you imagine what observations could have been designed by Dr. Brown to test her ideas?

Scientific study by researchers based on observations of baby crying has already had many benefits, including better diagnosing of illness in small infants, developing a better understanding of infant personality development, and decreasing parental abuse or neglect of infants. Think about the simple source of scientists' perceptions—just a baby crying. Then think about the possible usefulness of their work.

Precisely and carefully noticing any aspect of life is an essential step for understanding one's life. For example, your awareness of your body and its normal and abnormal conditions helps you determine your state of health and when to seek medical advice.

Observation might enable you to use your body's sensory system in biofeedback techniques to help control tension or migraine headaches. Observing and evaluating body language can help you better understand friends and associates. A good test of this type of awareness is to turn it around and use it to imagine how others might see you. In all of these instances, you will be using your newly honed observational skills.

Finally, it is important for you to believe that you can see or sense something uniquely—whether for private pleasure and happiness, or possibly to discover something worth sharing with others. Don't wait for someone else to get you started by suggesting a project or something to examine. Find your own individual "child's eye" and "window" from which to observe the world.

Summary

☞   Situations and conditions affect your observational experiences.

☞   Your willingness to explore and observe is an inherent quality from childhood.

☞   Vicarious sensory information can stunt your observational growth.

☞   You should properly evaluate observations.

☞   Sensory efforts vary in intensity. Methods exist that can be used to increase this sensitivity.

☞   Your sensory skills of observation can be developed by using certain techniques.

☞   Ideas, beliefs, and activities can convert observations into poignant accounts and creative bridges that make civilizations possible.

Observation more than books, experience rather than persons, are the prime educators.

–Amos Bronson Alcott

All our knowledge begins with senses, proceeds then to understanding, and ends with reason.

–Immanuel Kant

To acquire knowledge, one must study; but to acquire wisdom, one must observe.

–Marilyn vos Savant

Minor things can become moments of great revelation when encountered for the first time.

–Margot Fonteyn

People who don't work with primary sources don't understand reality.

–Franklin Burroughs

What is a scientist after all? It is a curious man looking through a keyhole, the keyhole of nature, trying to know what's going on.

– Jacques Cousteau

Your Ideas

That is what learning is. You should suddenly understand some-thing you've understood all your life, but in a new way.

– Doris Lessing

Your Ideas

_____

_____

_____

_____

_____

_____

_____

_____

_____

_____

_____

_____

_____

_____

_____

_____

_____

_____

_____

Never get so fascinated by the extraordinary that you forget the ordinary.   **– Magdalen Nabb**

Chapter 4

Creative Thought Processes

People who lovingly work with wood often say that each board is different. Not just because one is pine and another is walnut, but because the grain pattern in each board is unique.

The pattern tells the story of the tree's life. Did the sapling pine start out wedged between rocks? Was there a nearby overhanging wolf tree 📖 that limited the pine's growth because of the shadowed sun and shared root space? Did a mauling storm cause a torn limb? Was there a bacterial attack? Did the wolf tree finally topple allowing the pine to reach its crown out into an open sky? Each event shaped the pattern and texture of the wood.

Whereas a tree bears visible marks of its life experiences, people more often bear hidden recordings of their experiences. How? The way people think, their memory of history, their reaction to everyday events—all these become their internal markings.

Unlike the pine tree, your mobility, unique sensory system, and thinking ability make your process of living more complex. You see, feel, hear, image, construct, create, and travel through a web of unique personal experiences. This activity shapes and marks you as you seek favorable conditions for your growth and life. One of these beneficial conditions—the equivalent of the pine tree seeking sunlight—is the use of your creative abilities. As you speak, write, and otherwise share your insights with people, you receive many benefits, including a joyous sense of fulfillment and increased knowledge. Even the self-enlightenment that accompanies creative activity can be extraordinary; this is a wonderful incentive for continuing efforts to seek original expression of ideas.

For people who are creative, reaching toward personal expression within a culture is very much like the pine tree reaching toward sunlight. There is a common human need to use creativity to enliven and enhance daily life. As you seek your own personal expression, you may write, speak, or act creatively, and thus share and interpret life experiences. You may compare, rummage through a memory of words, open your mouth, seize a pen, and extend yourself into a cultural opening, like the pine tree reaching for the sky. These attempts to manage your own thoughts make you very special—a human being with creative possibilities.

Some human beings are limited by living narrowly, exposed to little outside experience of different people, places, or ideas. They are confined like the rock-bound pine. Some may feel overwhelmed by the abilities or activities of others and may be unable to reach out for their own share of "space" or recognition—like the pine in the shadow of the wolf tree. Some people have a physical disability or an illness that has left its mark. Yet, it is important to remember that all life events can be handled positively, creatively, and as learning opportunities. As long as you live, you are a carrier of possibilities and an instrument of self-development—especially when you participate in life with a cheerful, open-minded attitude, ready to learn.

Bristlecone pine trees, four thousand years old, must put forth new growth each year or they die. Your life, likewise, is dependent upon continuous growth—in the sense that pushing outward with your intellect and senses keeps you more fully alive. You may have heard the expression, "The sky is the limit," meaning that you can accomplish almost anything you desire since the limit is so high. Your accomplishments, whether simple or complex, prove that you are alive as a vibrant, mentally alert, creative human being.

Most knowledge arrives via our senses, and people vary greatly in the sensitivity of their sensory thresholds or how well they use those senses. Some persons have actual sensory disabilities and make use of aids such as eyeglasses or hearing aids which, coupled with creative thinking, help them achieve despite their handicap. For example, Beethoven 📖 contrived ᕐ a way to feel vibrations from loudly played music that enabled him to continue composing music despite his deafness.

Whatever your sensory abilities, the more you expand your experiences and your ability to observe, the more likely you are to be able to think expansively and creatively. There is always something to find, observe, or create; immense opportunities exist for discovery.

But where do you find original challenges? Anywhere and everywhere! Creative thinking can involve making, fixing, or describing something. Out of the woven tapestry ᕐ of everyday experiences, you can isolate distinct questions, puzzles, or problems to solve.

Suppose you want to describe your home to a distant relative in a new and unusual way. You could consider using photographs, a written description, or a scale model. You begin thinking about how these portray your home. All of these methods depend primarily on sight, and your relative is blind. The scale model comes closest to being useful because she could touch and feel it, but you think you can do something better. So you make a tape recording that portrays your passage through your house. The sounds include changes in your voice as well as in the sounds of footsteps on carpet versus linoleum, a radio playing, your younger brother crying—along with other descriptive comments, such as the number of steps taken in each room or your descriptions of items in each room. Instead of using the scale model, you developed a more original solution to your problem. Sometimes better solutions result without exploring traditional ideas.

Creativity requires thinking about things in new and different ways. When you think about a problem, use some fantasizing processes. Doodle pictures. Write a single sentence description. Ask questions. Why does this exist? When does this occur? Who needs this? Why? Then slide everything into your subconscious and let it incubate. Allow a period of gestation ↺. Go to sleep. Listen to some music. Rest. Turn to other matters. Your subconscious may deliver a solution, perhaps even at 2:00 a.m. Be prepared with paper and pencil by your bedside. Many scientists and artists have gotten solutions to problems in this way.

Work at feeding your subconscious, continually and with as extensive a list of comestibles ↺ as is possible. Experience everything deeply and widely, and you will increase your opportunities to be creative. For example, you might view Duchamp's painting, *Nude Descending a Staircase* 📖 and, without recognizing the source of inspiration, subsequently figure out a new and better way to guide blind people. While skiing, you might hear a particular sound effect as your skis swish rhythmically in the snow. Later, the sound becomes part of a symphonic passage—its source unidentified. Your background should be rich in "wild" or random information for future use. In addition, you need to know how to find and use information resources that are particular to your interests.

As Dr. Louis Pasteur said, "Chance favors the prepared mind." You need to be in good mental condition, always prepared to seize an elusive new idea.

Mental Conditioning

The following activities may help you keep in good mental condition. Try to use one or more of them regularly.

- Solve puzzles or mental games (charades, chess, Scrabble, crossword puzzles)
- Write short stories, poems, or music. Paint or sculpt.
- Maintain a creative interest in some special area. Attend relevant events.
- Carefully observe and describe something on a regular basis (faces, sky, comic strips, buildings, etc.).
- Imagine ways to improve situations around you. Note dissatisfaction with things as they are—cheerfully and creatively.

- Try to consider a question or problem of personal interest for 20-30 minutes without veering *∽* mentally.
- Try to find relationships between two very different objects. For example, pick some object and think of how it relates to some other object. This mental "doodling" usually begins with a thoughtful description of the objects. The most obvious properties will probably occur to you first. You picture the objects in your "mind's eye," then you search for similarities or differences that exist for these objects. Somewhere in this process, your background knowledge is being searched for congruent *∽* information relative to your descriptions. You continue to manipulate this information until there arises an "aha!" connection that is interesting, strange, or mentally arresting. A chain of thought develops with one idea producing another. This is a playful process, which may or may not yield any so-called useful ideas. The most important result is your increased awareness of the diversity in objects, your ability to think creatively, and possibly a developing awareness of looking more closely at your surroundings.

    For example, consider a chair and a raisin, two very different objects, and the following simplified chain of thought that is shown in the following sequence. The use of an exclamation point (!) indicates an unusual "aha!" connection with the preceding entries in this sample of one person's chain of thought.

  - Chair, wooden
  - Raisin, wrinkled
  - Wrinkles carved on a chair (Aha!)
  - Raisins
  - Raisin pie (Aunt Ella's)
  - Plump raisins

- Raisin, grape
- Grapevine, woody
- Chair made of old grapevines (Aha!)
- Grapes, picking
- A chair device to pick grapes (Aha!)

The process uses divergent thinking. Notice that critical judgment is suspended in this playful mental meandering ꙮ. To practice this process, pick words as randomly as possible. Flip through a dictionary to choose words, or trade words with a challenging companion. The most important result of this exercise is your increased awareness of the diversity in objects, your ability to think creatively, and possibly a developing habit of looking more closely at your surroundings.

- Use brainstorming techniques 📖 on a routine basis when you are attempting to solve problems. Allow yourself to experience an intense, internal reverie ꙮ where you consider solutions. Record all ideas, as many as possible—the wild ones, the improbable ones, and the fit-together-with-something-else ones. Make no judgments as to value during this process. You might find checklists of words—such as these shown below which are designed to help creative thinking— useful in triggering your ideas for solutions. You may also want to try to develop your own checklist, similar to the "Possible Science Checklist" shown below, but specially suited to your area of interest and your experience. Use your personal notebook or the blank pages at the end of this chapter to record such personal checklists to use when you are faced with situations that particularly require creative thinking.

Possible *General* Checklist		Possible *Science* Checklist	
substitute	input	optical	alloy
magnify	shape	electrical	reaction
minify	time	orientation	specification
reverse	group	tolerance	function
combine	custom	symmetry	charge
function	place	magnetic	shape

For example, suppose you are writing a short story and cannot find a way to account for your hero's absence during a critical scene. You might use the "General Checklist" to find alternate solutions such as the ones that follow.

Substitute He had to take his brother's place as an usher.

Magnify He is in jail, accused of stealing an elephant.

Minify Heedless of time, he is playing with his grandson.

Or perhaps for a science project you are to solve a problem of soil erosion. You might use the science checklist to creatively come up with some possible solutions.

Optical Can I actually see greater erosion or changes in the dark colored soils?

Electrical Do soil particle charges change after rainfall? Is this due to acidity?

Orientation Is there a pattern of ridged surfaces?

Creative processes such as these can be used to solve problems or to discover or invent something new. One good idea may trigger two others, and a chain reaction ensues. Trading ideas in group sessions often can be more productive than working alone.

The opportunity to discover and know is nearly boundless. If you do "walk into a wall," turn around and go the other way, or find a door, or poke a hole in the ceiling and grab a ladder. With practice and training, everyone can be more creative. Use your creativity. When you appreciate the vastness of the human imagination, become excited by the unknown, use all of your senses and abilities to explore, and share your creativity with others, you become beautifully marked by these efforts.

Summary

☞ Thinking processes are complex and personally unique.

☞ Natural limits exist for knowledge and accomplishments, but they are "sky-high."

☞ The extent of your related knowledge affects problem-solving processes.

☞ A subconscious "ripening" or incubation of a problem frequently produces answers.

☞ Creative efforts will almost surely make you more creative.

☞ Some specific procedures can be useful generators of ideas for problem-solving.

☞ A positive outlook improves chances of success in creative thinking.

Imagination is the highest kite one can fly.
– Lauren Bacall

The shrewd guess, the fertile hypothesis, the courageous leap to a tentative conclusion—these are valuable coins of the thinker at work.
– Jerome Bruner

To walk on water, wait until it freezes.
– Jeffrey Woodruff Livingston

A problem is not solved in a laboratory. It is solved in some fellow's head, and all the apparatus is for is to get his head turned around so he can see the thing right.
– Charles F. Kettering

When a person never changes his mind, it's usually a pretty good indication that he's stopped thinking.
– Laura Van Wormer

To have ideas is to gather flowers; to think is to weave them into garlands.
– Anne Sophie Swetchine

Your Ideas

If one is lucky, a solitary fantasy can totally transform one million realities.   — **Maya Angelou**

Your Ideas

Our thought is the key which unlocks the doors of the world.
– Samuel McChord Crothers

Chapter 5

Speed Reading

Reading is an intellectual art, a canvassing of human thought, and a tool useful in shaping your life. If you read successfully, you can quickly recognize letter and word patterns, and you will associate them with personal experiences. This produces mental images and ideas. If you are not able to read clearly and quickly, you may avoid the act of reading altogether and thus miss the joys that can come from reading.

Reading rapidly is desirable, but reading faster and remembering less is traveling in the wrong direction. Therefore, speed reading means reading as fast as possible, considering your ability and the type of material, while retaining enough to have made the reading worthwhile. If you have not already learned this, it should be a relief to learn that good readers seldom read every word; this is one way to increase your reading rate.

You can develop and use different strategies for a variety of reading purposes. For example, you won't read a science book the same way you read the sports page in the newspaper. For the science book, you might first scan all the headings and bold print words to become familiar with key concepts. Then you might skim each section quickly for an overview of ideas. Finally, you will go back to more thoroughly read each section for understanding. For the sports page, you will likely read quickly and then may stop after the second line. You may only need to know how a certain player scored. You read, looking for the score, and then turn the page.

Always consider your purpose for reading and the amount of time you have available. President Kennedy allowed himself only a half an hour to skim through three newspapers every morning at breakfast. With limited time, he still wanted to scan the headlines and relevant articles. Whatever the purpose for your reading, learning and practicing speed reading techniques will allow you to read and retain more material. You will be able to double, and in some cases triple, your reading speed and comprehension from what it is now if you practice using some of the techniques described in this chapter.

Here are some helpful suggestions for reading improvement:

Physical Conditions

- Make sure that vision problems have been corrected to the best extent possible; have regular eye examinations.
- Choose reading surroundings that are quiet and not intrusive.
- Use lighting that minimizes glare.
- Set up your reading area with paper, pen, pencils, dictionary, and any other needed materials.
- If the reading is very demanding, take a five-minute break every half-hour. Walk around, look at distant objects, close your eyes, listen to some music, or do some minor chore.
- Sit in a chair that provides good back support and does not promote sleepiness.

Eye Span and Return Sweeps

Do you know how to increase efficiency by increasing your reading eye span? Your present eye span may only allow you to see one or two medium length words of average type size; for example, "written word." With a little practice, you can enlarge your eye span to look at four or five words at a time. Make a slotted card that can frame typical three-to-four word lengths. By sliding it along, you can become accustomed to viewing a longer line of type on the page.

Going from one-word recognition to three-word recognition more than triples your reading comprehension speed. Why? The cluster of words can produce ideas and images that are more complex and meaningful. For example, consider your responses sequentially to the following: *bright*, then *bright blue*, then finally, *bright, blue balloon.* If each word is responded to singly, the mind "clutters" with unnecessary images, and reading is slowed as a result.

You can also improve return eye sweeps; these occur when the eye moves from the end of one line to the beginning of the next. Slow or inaccurate sweeps decrease speed. One simple way to improve sweep is to hold a piece of paper under each line, allowing you to only see one line at a time. When you finish the line, move the paper down. This will help train your eyes to sweep correctly across to the next line. An alternate activity to increase reading speed is to hold a piece of paper above each line, and then to increase the rate at which you move the paper down the page.

Other rapid reading techniques using eye-hand coordination are described in *Speed Reading, The Easy Way* by Howard Stephen Berg and Marcus Conyers (1998). They show that it is possible to increase reading rate from 200 words per minute to at least 2,000 words per minute.

Improving and Expanding Your Vocabulary

If you have a small vocabulary, your reading is impeded ᏕᎠ. You must either skip each unknown word, with potential loss of meaning, or stop to check it in a dictionary. Here are some suggestions for improving and expanding your vocabulary:

- Obtain a dictionary.
- In your personal notebook, keep a list of new vocabulary words from your readings.

- Make homemade flash cards with the new word on one side and the definition on the other side. (Also, note the pronunciation.) Flip through these cards once or twice a week.

- Try to incorporate your new words into your conversations and writing.

Visualization

"Think while you read" in order to turn printed ideas into vivid personal pictures. Think of exciting stories you have read in the past and the pictures of all the characters you created in your "mind's eye." Do you remember Winnie the Pooh or Long John Silver? Those characters are easy to recall and the stories were easy to read because of visual pictures you created in your mind.

Do the same sort of picture imaging with all of your reading. Associate technical or more difficult words with other terms that can be transformed into pictures. If you are reading about something so foreign to you that images cannot be formed, obtain supplemental material. For example, when reading about Medieval Europe and the Knights of the Round Table, you might find a book with illustrations of typical castle architecture helpful.

Reading improvement also occurs if you can decrease vocalization (sounding out words half-aloud or forming words with your lips) and instead concentrate only on sight-reading. This is a much quicker way to read, but requires that you practice keeping your lips still.

Another reading shortcut comes from developing quick visual familiarity with the style and content of the material before reading it thoroughly. For example, prefaces and other introductory materials often provide information about the overall framework as well as the writer's purpose and point of view—all essential to your understanding of your reading. Very experienced rapid readers scan for key words or focus their sight on the centers of paragraphs. Then, they either visually reject the surplus words or note them peripherally ᧡. This can be risky, however, especially with technical material. Initially, this style of reading is difficult, but its mastery can be useful where precise awareness of content is not necessary, such as in reading fiction.

Paper and Pen Reading

When you read, keep a pen or pencil handy to make notes. Gilbert Keith Chesterton and George Bernard Shaw maintained an unusual correspondence with each other by exchanging books that they annotated in the margins. Their comments were often peppery because of their conflicting philosophies. This type of correspondence became practical only because they personally owned the books they used to mentally challenge each other.

- If you own a book that has limited value such as a paperback or used book, you may want to underline or use a yellow marker to highlight key ideas. You may want to make additional marginal notations for review purposes.

- If you don't own the book, you may want to use notebooks, file cards, or a computer to record valuable ideas or to make comments about the content. You could also write comments on "sticky notes" and place them on the actual page.

Paper and pen reading has a number of benefits. The *physical* activity of writing actually helps keep your mind alert. Also, "smart laziness," or efficiency, ensues. Condensing one hundred words of original content to just a sentence or a five-word phrase may make an important idea more memorable.

As you read, ask yourself questions. What do I know about this? What should I know? Why does the author say this? Do I agree with the author? Why or why not? Asking questions as you read makes the reading go easier and faster, and you will remember better what you read. This questioning technique also improves your understanding of the relevance of the content to your life.

Selection and Material

Choose your reading material wisely by considering possible returns for time spent. Even when reading for pleasure, the content can yield knowledge or perspective (in addition to reading practice).

Select material that really interests you and has reasonable print size. The writing should have a style and vocabulary that is slightly challenging but not overwhelming. Obtain suggestions for your reading from knowledgeable friends, librarians, bibliographies, and book reviews. Go to a library and browse through the "new books" display, or look in the stacks at books in areas that are unknown to you; read book jackets, and leaf through randomly selected passages. If you have always read mysteries or science fiction, consider expanding your reading interests to include biography or history.

Practice

As with any skill, reading requires repetitive experiences to reach satisfactory performance levels, *especially* if you are a poor reader. To improve, you should set aside time for practice. Consciously use the ideas listed above to increase your speed.

Mnemonics

Since reading depends so much upon memory, memory aids can enhance your reading skills. You can create a pattern or system to help you remember the new material. You might remember an unusual term because it sounds like something else with which you are more familiar (e.g., hone and bone), has a similar beginning to a related word (e.g., mnemonics, memory), or has a recognizable form in another language (e.g., prisoner, prisonier). Eventually it will be mentally simpler and more efficient to have direct recall of a term's meaning, but using a mnemonic scheme can help at the outset. As a suggestion, obtain a book on memory or mnemonics from a library, and try some of the exercises.

A reader with limited life experience often finds it difficult to understand the significance of what is being read. Of course, we do broaden our life experience through reading, but such experience is second-hand and often lacks depth and perspective. There is no simple solution to this problem. By acquiring first-hand diverse experience at every opportunity, you will broaden your base of understanding. Whatever your extent of life experience, the most important thing is that your mind is thinking and processing as you read.

Summary

To improve reading skills:

❏ Check physical conditions such as lighting.

❏ Increase your eye span.

❏ Expand your vocabulary.

❏ Turn printed words into pictures in your mind's eye.

❏ Decrease or eliminate vocalization; avoid reading "half aloud."

❏ Use scanning techniques.

❏ Write comments and questions as you read.

❏ As you read, ask questions about content to increase your understanding of relevance and to enhance your memory.

❏ Set aside time to practice reading.

❏ Choose wisely what you read.

❏ Schedule regular library visits.

❏ Use mnemonics or other memory aids.

❏ Expand your own personal life experiences and background of information.

Some books are to be tasted, others to be swallowed, and some few to be chewed and digested: that is, some books are to be read only in parts, others to be read, but not curiously, and some few to be read wholly, and with diligence and attention.

– Francis Bacon

Just the knowledge that a good book is awaiting one at the end of a long day makes that day happier.

– Kathleen Norris

The big advantage of a book is it's very easy to rewind. Close it and you're right back at the beginning.

– Jerry Seinfeld

Reading without reflecting is like eating without digesting.

– Edmund Burke

If we encountered a man of rare intellect, we should ask him what books he read.

– Ralph Waldo Emerson

The greatest gift is the passion for reading. It is cheap, it consoles, it distracts, it excites, it gives you knowledge of the world and experience of a wide kind. It is a moral illumination.

– Elizabeth Hardwick

Your Ideas

_____

_____

_____

_____

_____

_____

_____

_____

_____

_____

_____

_____

_____

_____

_____

_____

_____

_____

_____

_____

_____

Reading furnishes our mind only with materials of knowledge; it is thinking that makes what we read ours.   **– John Locke**

Your Ideas

_____

_____

_____

_____

_____

_____

_____

_____

_____

_____

_____

_____

_____

_____

_____

_____

_____

_____

_____

You can think your pain and heartbreak are unprecedented in the history of the world, but then you read. It was books that taught me that the things that tormented me most were the very things that connected me with all the people who were alive, or who had ever been alive.   **– James Baldwin**

Chapter 6
Enthusiasm and Confidence

The world is full of avenues for exploration. For example, you may have discovered the richness of the American art pottery movement, or the challenges of painting miniatures, or an unusual toccata ♫. Perhaps you have invented a new product, or you see a way to solve a community problem. Enthusiastically, you share your excitement with everyone, but sometimes get rebuffed and thus discover one of the few drawbacks of being really excited about anything.

But suppose one day you decide that you have proceeded far enough with an idea to seek advice from several experts. The first praises your scholarship, intuition, and discoveries. The second points out some problems, errors in judgment, and flaws in reasoning. When you think about these conflicting opinions, you see new ways to approach your topic. After talking with these experts, you have even more confidence in your work, are no longer hesitant, and remain enthusiastic. The first expert's encouraging words prevented you from giving up too soon when your work became difficult. The second expert's critique helped you develop needed changes. Most importantly, you retained your confidence and self-esteem throughout this process, which allowed you to also retain your enthusiasm and creative effort.

Enthusiasm and Well-Being

Having enthusiasm is an important part of your well-being. Observe people you know. Which ones are absorbed in some interest? What effect does this excitement have upon their life? As you study the lives of famous people through biographies and autobiographies, does their enthusiasm seem obvious? Are their hobbies, multiple talents, community involvement, or career efforts central to that person's lifestyle? For example, Franklin D. Roosevelt 📖 was an avid ✍ stamp collector. Thomas Jefferson 📖 had many strong interests, including architecture and gardening. Hobbies not only enrich your leisure time, but they also may develop into full-time careers later. Among the people you know, are there any who have hobbies? Contrast their lives with those who do not. What do you conclude? Whether your enthusiasm is toward a hobby or toward some other endeavor, enthusiasm provides power for your interests. Under the right circumstances, enthusiasm is contagious and can motivate groups. How do you get enthusiasm? Some people seem only to catch second-hand enthusiasms; they never start their own. They attend popular events, seek occupations that have crowd approval, and read magazines and newspapers to determine what they like. They wear clothing with labels as status symbols to bolster their confidence. Others have enthusiasm generated from within. They plan events that excite them, follow their personal interests, and are happy with themselves. Try to have that kind of enthusiasm.

Self-Generated Enthusiasm

To nurture your own self-generated enthusiasm, let your self emerge without listening only to the interjected ✍ voices of parents, authority, tradition, the experts, or the status-seekers. Stay as close as possible to your own inner world. Believe in fresh sight, accept the possibility that reasoning can be flawed and that facts can be added to, changed, and rearranged. Transcend the limitations that reason and tradition are always trying to impose. Would you describe Picasso as being a "second-hand enthusiast"? With his prodigious ✍ output, his innovative adventuring, and his hearty enjoyment of life, "primogenitor ✍ enthusiast" is a better label.

Primogenitor, or self-generated, enthusiasm requires intensive efforts of introspection, self-discovery, and self-development. Look at the enthusiasm and confidence of salespeople who depend upon their personal growth, their belief in themselves, their product line, and their ability to understand their customers. Good salespeople know a lot. The skills of relating to people are the art of successful sales. Good salespeople are creative. Supersalesman Joe Girard 📖 shares many of his sales techniques in several books worth reading.

Nurturing Enthusiasm

But how do you nurture and maintain enthusiasm once your initial response dwindles? Your failure to be enthusiastic may occur because certain activities are no longer enlightening or give you intellectual stimulation. Even when everything is bleakest and darkest, you can find resources within or without that can rekindle the excitement. For example, suppose you have always enjoyed cryptography ✍. But lately, you find it a dead-end, no longer challenging or fun. Yet you really do not wish to let it go; some part of you is still attached and interested. Perhaps you can add cryptography to something else in order to create a new interest. For example, combine it with literature to write a novel or detective story, or use a page in your journal to brainstorm other combinations. If you are certain that your love affair with codes is over, it is probably time for you to find something new and to turn your attention elsewhere.

Beware of being the dilettante ✍ enthusiast—quick to embrace and quick to reject items to explore. Allow your interests to consume you for some significant period of time. Otherwise, you may never experience "seeing below the surface" and are far less likely to be an innovator ✍.

At the other extreme, you might be tempted to hold on to your interest and enthusiasm beyond the point of reasonableness. When it approaches the comfortableness of an old shoe, it is time to go shopping. Gerald M. Loeb 📖, a brilliant stock market investor, used a formula to cut his market losses to a minimum. He applied the ratchet effect (a ratchet prevents reversal of motion); when his investments *began* to slip backward, he froze his gains and got out of the market. The same principle can be used for investments of self and time. When something begins to pall ↩, give it critical examination and consider applying a ratchet.

But what about tasks in front of you, particularly if they are unchosen, unloved, and uninteresting? Can you summon enthusiasm for things you do not care about? Why not? If you can regard enthusiasm as a feasible alternative to boredom, hatred, or distaste, you will have the beginning of a good solution to such mundane tasks. Use your creative wit. Dream up excitement. Find relationships between the present situation and something you care about. Fantasize. Construct images. Regard the present as an opportunity to observe accurately. However, if even with your best effort some matters cannot be greeted enthusiastically, so be it.

Your enthusiasms should be selective. Without contrast, enthusiasms fail to please and inform. As long as something excites you, storms your entire being, and holds you enthralled ↩, all is well.

One special kind of enthusiasm can totally engulf you. It is the zeal associated with a **cause**. The etymology ↩ of enthusiasm is based on Greek terms meaning divinely inspired; all of that archaic ↩ meaning is related to religious emotions and inspirations. Modern causes may or may not have religious origins, but they are sources of enthusiasm nonetheless. Some popular causes include environmental issues, racial and social discrimination, animal rights, rebuilding of cities, and saving historical landmarks. Find a cause that suits you and your available time. Work at it. You will meet people, gain valuable skills, and feel good inside. You may even find your life's work developing from this cause. Even better, *choose* a cause that is associated with your career interests. Consider your volunteer efforts to be an enthusiastic form of community tithing ↩.

When It's Hard To Be Enthusiastic

What about "down days" when you find it hard to be enthusiastic about things that are usually pleasurable? When the effort to enjoy doing pleasant tasks is difficult, remember that everyone has "down days." Assuming that you are not physically tired (perhaps from lack of sleep—then take a nap), the best advice is to get busy, take a brisk walk, clean your desk, or make something. One young man solved this problem in a unique way. He kept the ingredients for homemade chili on hand and made a large batch whenever "down days" occurred. Then he called friends and invited them to come and dine. By reaching out and becoming involved in the outside world, he was able to overcome the blankness or emptiness of these occasional days.

What if your "down days" are more than occasional? You may be suffering from depression, a condition that can be remediated by medical or psychological attention. Talk to your family. Get help from your family doctor. Sometimes professional help is needed to jumpstart your life to regain your interests and to be enthusiastic again. Then, once more, you will be able to trust your ability to assess events realistically, to find satisfaction in using your ability, and to take pleasure in being creative.

An open society does not grant nor refuse the right to be enthusiastic. You can pick your "thing" just about as freely as you can pick flowers in spring. But you may not have as much freedom in gaining societal respect and support for your enthusiasms. Here are some valuable tips:

- Ideas are more quickly accepted from people who fit certain patterns of behavior and appearance—those who have the "right image" or the "right stuff." People may not hear a message because they are distracted by the messenger.

- Sometimes new ideas are opposed by others simply because they challenge the tradition and the *status quo*

∾. Is it possible to change this regrettable circumstance? Yes, history is rife ∾ with the denials of new beliefs by many creative persons particularly if they were women, renegade artists, minorities, and political dissidents—until their determined persistence, persuasiveness, and enthusiasm overwhelmed the opposition. Can you persist? You may want to investigate all possible avenues of publicity to keep your cause alive. You could write letters and articles, meet influential people, join organizations, use the Internet, organize public events—all hard work. Strong enthusiasm is worth effort. Great enthusiasm is worth exceptional effort.

- Your interests and enthusiasms describe and measure you. They tell your size—not in feet or pounds but in feats and sounds. Out of all possible interests, what have you chosen and why? What have you done with your choice? Have you confined your passion to a private sanctum ∾ , or have you shared it? What deeds, songs, or sayings have you set forth?

- Have you managed to make your life a network of enthusiasms? Do these touch other humans in accord with eternal verities ∾ such as truth, beauty, goodness, and all the other finest ideals of human conception? If they do, your enthusiasm will bring you self-confidence and assurance. Your works will not simply be a toccata—you will have let loose a symphony! Now let loose your personal reactions to the ideas in this chapter in the blank pages here or in your personal notebook.

Summary

☞   Sharing enthusiasms is a risky but essential and rewarding process.

☞   Some enthusiasms arise from popular sources; others arise from personal effort.

☞   Self-generated enthusiasms develop in response to intense self-search and open-mindedness.

☞   Enthusiasms can be short-lived, humdrum, or exchanged.

☞   Causes can provide unusual inspiration.

☞   Pursued enthusiasms yield confidence.

Words of Wisdom

If you are all wrapped up in yourself, you are overdressed.

– Kate Halverson

If you wish in this world to advance
Your merits you're bound to enhance;
You must stir it and stump it,
And blow your own trumpet,
Or, trust me, you haven't a chance.

– W. S. Gilbert

You grow up the day you have your first real laugh at yourself.

– Ethel Barrymore

Somehow I can't believe that there are any heights that can't be scaled by a man who knows the secret of making dreams come true. This special secret, it seems to me, can be summarized in four C's. They are curiosity, confidence, courage, and constancy, and the greatest of these is confidence. When you believe in a thing, believe in it all the way, implicitly and unquestionably.

– Walt Disney

Confidence comes not from always being right but from not fearing to be wrong.

– Peter T. McIntyre

There is real magic in enthusiasm.... It gives warmth and good feeling to all your personal relationships.

– Norman Vincent Peale

Your Ideas

_____

_____

_____

_____

_____

_____

_____

_____

_____

_____

_____

_____

_____

_____

_____

_____

_____

_____

_____

_____

Nothing great was ever achieved without enthusiasm.
– Ralph Waldo Emerson

Your Ideas

Self-confidence is the first requisite to great undertakings.
– Samuel Johnson

Chapter 7
Decision
Making

Suppose you are attending a party that has become boring. You consider your options:

- leaving
- figuring out how you can add some excitement
- getting someone else to join with you to make it more interesting
- inciting someone else to "make it more lively"

Which is the "right" choice? Which would you choose? There might be alternative solutions, but there is no "right" answer to the party problem. This is true of most other problems or situations requiring decisions as well. You make your decision based on choices that are consonant ᧡ with your personal beliefs and values, your knowledge, cultural experiences, interests, and personality. The decision may be easy or difficult, and it may be based on previous experiences making different types of decisions. Sometimes a decision is made out of habit (e.g., "I've always done it that way."), and sometimes people avoid making a decision at all (which is its own kind of decision). Making the decision not to decide keeps the issue in limbo ᕗ or allows others to step in and make the decision for you, which may not be what you want. Hopefully, though, most of your decisions will be active and thoughtful ones. And like other abilities, your decision making skills will improve with practice.

You Are the Constant in Your Decisions

Throughout your efforts to reach any decision, there will be one constant presence—you, with all of your various experiences and your personality. Using the same information, events, and circumstances, would someone else arrive at the same decision as you? Possibly. Possibly not. For example, a journalist narrowly escapes being killed in a building collapse. The variability of "eyewitness accounts" concerning that event are more apparent to him now because he was directly involved in the situation himself. As a result of this dramatic event, he decides to change his style of reporting to rely less on eyewitness accounts, and more on solid facts. This reporter's experience and knowledge, derived from this one incident, also influences his decision to write more investigative pieces in the future. Eventually, he uses his new fact-finding skills to write articles that contribute to the revision of regulations governing the local construction industry. Do you think you would have been affected in the same way by this experience? Will events in your life affect your future decisions?

The way you view life and customarily respond to events and experiences also influences your decisions. Are you future-oriented? Can you look beyond today and consider both the short- and long-term consequences of a decision you are contemplating? Are you capable of making good decisions that run counter to common expectations? What is your balance between being courageous and being foolhardy? Your personality is showing!

Your personality certainly contributes to your style of decision making. Recall the party scenario from the beginning of this chapter. Which action would you choose? Are you shy or introverted? If so, you might decide to leave the dull party. Are you an instigator

&⁀? Then you might decide to get someone else to start a new game or activity. Are you a socializer or good at sharing? Perhaps you and a friend would put on a great act. Your personality will influence the manner with which you approach a choice.

In the job market, your personality may also influence the way you go about searching for a job. If you are shy and introverted, you might decide to simply send your resume &⁀ to companies or to use the services of an employment agency. If you are social, good at sharing, and someone who enjoys personal involvement, you might decide to phone companies for more information or seek out people who work there. If you are extroverted and assertive, you might decide to call the company and directly request an appointment to discuss job opportunities.

Decisions are also based on information, either spoken or written. But it is important to realize that information often can be inaccurately perceived. Ichak Adizes, in his book *Mastering Change: The Power of Mutual Trust and Respect in Personal Life, Family Life, Business and Society,* has many interesting comments concerning listening skills, such as: "We have learned how to separate feeling from hearing from listening. Consider the expression 'tune out.' We treat people like a radio station we don't want to listen to."

In addition to understanding functional mishearing, you need to be sensitive to tone of voice, customary verbal style, and body language in order to evaluate communications that could affect your decisions. Even with the best of intentions, people do not always mean what they say. Arguing which a person uses as a means to reinforce an opinion can instead appear as an expression of disagreement.

Rude people and other personalities can influence your decisions, sometimes irritating you so much as to prevent your wise response to their requests or even to preclude &⁀ your acceptance of needed information from them. When this happens, try to concentrate on solving problems in a way that is most beneficial to you and least harmful (perhaps even beneficial) to them. Getting caught up in emotional reactions to other people can limit your vision and can lead to poor choices.

Factors that Favor Good Decisions

Before approaching any decision, you may want to think about factors that favor making good decisions. This list includes your ability to:

• Know and care about yourself and others.

• Sense opportunities within changing conditions.

• Keep an optimistic view of the future.

• Identify and accept good ideas, valid information, and advice.

• Develop many and diverse ideas.

• Tolerate others who are different from you, and learn from them.

• Be aware of your feelings and values.

• Believe in the goodness within you and others.

• Accept responsibility with mature assurance.

• Benefit from failure by learning how to succeed next time.

Few people can be all of the above even some of the time. But just being conscious of these ideas and attempting to include them in your approach to decisions can still make a significant difference in the end result. Perhaps you think you are too young, or too powerless to make a difference by your decisions. In fact, however, the most innovative changes in society have been spawned *᳒* by youth. Probably the most powerful "head of steam" ever created is young people trying to set on fire a world that, to them, is all wet. The need for good decisions has never been exhausted, and there will always be a need for them.

Some decisions are easy and almost automatic; others are difficult. Some problem situations require nearly instantaneous decisions. If you are in a situation that is potentially dangerous to your physical or mental health, you will no doubt decide to get out of the situation as quickly and safely as possible. This would happen if the situation involved physical danger such as an explosion, or was a situation involving people that had become either frightening or abusive.

Your everyday decisions usually are not made with much fore-thought. Frequently, you act out of habit when you greet people, choose food, or fill a coffee cup for a friend. Some of these decisions may seem trivial. However, there are consequences for all acts. A pleasant greeting tends to attract people to you—a basis for developing friendships. Good eating habits tend to keep you healthy. Some habits may not be beneficial. Decisions to smoke could lead to an addiction, which could result years later in painful death from lung cancer or emphysema. A review of your everyday habitual decisions can be revealing and helpful.

Other types of decisions allow a more leisurely approach, permitting you to gather facts and information before you decide and to use some creative thinking processes as you examine your options. A decision about whether to enter a contest or apply for a new job will require some time for gathering and analyzing data. One quick strategy for reviewing information in this type of decision making is simply to list the pros and cons of the decision in two columns on a sheet of paper. When you are finished, compare the lists and make your decision.

Most people have trouble making major decisions. What is a decision facing you now or in the future? Why is this decision important? What sort of process will you use to help you decide? Will it be random, or will it be deliberate and thoughtful? Think back on a good decision you have made. Why was it good? Think back to a poor decision you have made. What made it a poor decision?

5 Stages of Decision Making

The initiating force behind every decision is change. Changes in your life lead to the need for decisions—sometimes simple, sometimes complicated. Being able to sense changes as soon as they occur may help you develop unique and creative responses of lasting value. Thomas Edison's inventiveness often was in response to the changes in living conditions of his time.

Consider one of the simpler problems to solve. You want to go to the beach, but have no way to get there. What are your options? Using the following system might seem too complex for such a simple problem. But for more complex problems it can be quite helpful. Practice in using this system can give you an idea of its value in making real decisions about more difficult situations in the future.

**Stage 1
Define the Problem**

Decision making is essentially made up of five stages of thought. The first stage is understanding problems and opportunities, and is made up of a seemingly disconnected series of questions and reactions. Why is this happening now? How is this possible? What is involved? When do I have to act? This process is actually a preliminary defining of the problem by including an awareness of what it is, narrowing its dimensions, and realizing how it affects you and others.

Often it is essential to accurately identify the issue at hand before you attempt any further efforts. Wisely, you should also match your effort to the size and seriousness of the problem. To start the more complete process of defining, make a list of what you believe is the nature of the issue. Use as many as possible of the following "Describers" to assist you in this process.

- What has (or has not) happened that makes a decision necessary?
- Who has (or has not) changed in this situation?
- When did (or will) this situation occur?
- Where did (or does) this happen?
- Why is this a problem (or opportunity)?
- Do I have the authority to make a decision?
- Do I have the means to act if I make a decision?
- How quickly do I have to make a decision?
- What information or assistance do I need?

Try to divide a complicated situation into smaller pieces before using the "Describers." For example, suppose you are interested in buying a musical instrument to improve your career opportunities as a musician. Issues could include finding sufficient funds, locating an affordable and quality instrument, and determining how to use it to enhance your reputation. Imagine how the "Describers" might be utilized through each part of this problem. Try using the "Describers" with an issue that presently concerns you. Make a list of answers. Perhaps the answers seem sketchy, but remember, they can provide important structure for future action. By using the answers, you can create a time frame and realize your needs concerning this issue. This defining has another benefit—it keeps you active, focused, and moves the process along. If you have the flexibility, allow the problem to "rest" for a few days, while you gather conscious (and subconscious) ideas and information.

Collecting practical knowledge is essential in defining, as it is throughout all the stages of working on a decision. A mistake often made by decision makers is not using something because they aren't aware that it exists. For example, a person thinking about college may know that he does not have money for tuition, and he might decide not to apply for college because he is unaware that there are scholarships, grants, and tuition waivers. Information from other people can help you understand the nature and dimension of a problem that you are trying to define—especially when different ideas are shared freely in an atmosphere of mutual trust and respect. Your willingness to seek and use valid information from many sources makes you a better, more confident decision maker.

**Stage 2
Setting a Goal**

After working with the "Describers" and defining the problem or opportunity, what is next? What do you want to do about this issue? You need to select a specific goal, aim, or target if you are to attain a solution. This is stage two of the decision making process.

Perhaps you have heard the saying, "If you don't know where you want to go, you'll probably never get there." Setting goals is a way of getting things moving. One of the best methods for achieving goals later is to write them down now. Once you have established that you want to do something, your mind can begin planning how best to make it happen, even subconsciously. If you write that you want to spend a summer traveling in Europe, for example, your mind can now begin thinking and planning for that goal.

Frequently, little conscious effort has to be given to selecting appropriate goals because inwardly you constantly have access to helpful directing information and judging ability. Your most consistent guidance comes from basic principles that you have accepted as personally important. These principles, usually few in number, are those that you share with most of the people in your community. They could include such concepts as honor, justice, and integrity. From these concepts, you tend to develop many values that then help you establish specific goals. Occasional review of this entire personal system of principles and values is desirable. You might like to consider the thoughts of Rabbi Abraham Heschel who said, "If I am not for myself, who will be for me? And if I am only for myself, then who am I?"

Sometimes more than one goal is involved. In reviewing the example of buying a musical instrument, for example, you may find that many different goals are involved in helping you reach your final decision. Besides achieving a better career opportunity, perhaps you wish to earn more money, join a professional musician's group, earn the respect of family and friends, improve personal skill, or simply be happier. In most cases, good decisions favor the coincidence of reaching many goals.

In general, goals tend to fit into two categories—broadly encompassing and narrowly specific. A broadly encompassing goal might be to seek ways to enhance your happiness, select a career, or choose a mate. A narrowly specific goal could include completing a list of telephone calls you need to make by a certain date. If you value being prompt, you will make the telephone calls by a certain date. However, if making timely telephone calls will interrupt some event of great importance in keeping you happy, then the telephone calls will wait. There is a possible way to maintain your integrity—a principle that is important to you—in this situation. You would need to find someone else who is reliable and who can make the telephone calls on time.

Goals which merit the most serious consideration are those that could have a prolonged influence in the future upon you and others. However, life does not ensure the accuracy of predictions. Therefore the wise person remains alert to changing conditions and thoughtfully adjusts goals accordingly.

**Stage 3
Hypothesize Solutions**

These considerations of goals and the future are the background for the third stage in the decision making process. You have already defined your problem/opportunity, and have set goals. It is time to **hypothesize** in order to figure out potential solutions. After defining the issue and giving it time to "rest," perhaps you came up with some ideas. You may find that creative ideas can be triggered by visual information contained in illustrated books on unrelated topics. Begin by listing your alternative ideas—perhaps in your personal notebook, on a computer, or on a wall chart.

You may need to use some devices to nourish your imagination. Some people schedule creative thinking time and listen to music, while others need total quiet. Flipping through dictionaries, related (or unrelated) books, or magazines can help spark ideas. Ideas arrive like fireflies from the darkness of night. Enlightenment can occur suddenly, or it can elude you for days. Patience is an ally. Keep gathering information relative to your problem. Record all of your ideas—without judgment—until you have obtained a number of solutions that seem reasonable.

**Stage 4
Judgment by Ranking**

When you seem to have reached the limit of potential solutions, or when you are driven by time constraints, you have reached the fourth stage, judgment. You begin this stage by ranking your potential solutions according to how useful they are to you. In this preliminary sequence, you will be responding to a complex collection of personal values, emotions, intuition, knowledge, and experience. When your list is finished, take your first choice and check its usefulness by questioning how well it solves all aspects of the described situation. This examination may cause you to rearrange your ranking. For this evaluation, the following checklist (which particularly applies to creative effort) may be helpful.

- Is the amount of effort required reasonable?
- Is the amount of needed material or equipment reasonable?

- Will it produce timely results?
- Is it reversible? Can anything else be done if it doesn't work?
- Is it likely to produce new or unusually good results?
- Is it likely that you can get the needed equipment, money, publicity, etc.?
- Is it of low or high risk?
- Are there likely to be negative consequences?
- Is it likely to produce fewer problems than it solves?
- Is it likely to be useful in solving other problems or in creating other opportunities?
- Is it legal, moral, and ethical?
- Is it culturally acceptable, and does it matter?

You may wish to develop other checklists to help you in solving interpersonal or other specific problems. Use your checklist to evaluate the potential solutions, keeping in mind the possibility that you may already have a preconceived idea or even a personal bias. When possible, you might seek a second opinion or even feedback from a group of evaluators. What you are developing is a narrowing list of options.

You will probably develop a style of selection and, if successful, you will keep it. For example, one style might give first choice to the option that could produce a large payoff with little effort—even though it is an outside chance or long shot. Another style would make as your choice of last resort any selection that is irreversible. Review your decisions (and your style of decision making) on separate occasions, with some intervening time for reflection. Two good questions to ask yourself are:

1. What will be the first result of this option?
2. What will be the lasting result of this option?

Hopefully, your reflection will help you avoid using unwise decision making processes. Some particular examples of foolish or careless decision making approaches would include:

- I'll toss a coin.
- I'll do it the usual way; it has always worked.
- I'll jump right in before someone else does.
- I'll hope no one notices.
- I'll just do this; there is no other way.
- I'll try anything; something is bound to work.
- I'll do nothing and hope the problem goes away.

Stage 5
Making the Decision

As the number of options dwindle to only a few equally acceptable possibilities, you have arrived at the final, or fifth, stage—the **decision** itself, with perhaps an alternate choice. The final selection is made by reviewing all of your knowledge of the present situation, while considering experience with previous decisions, and also thinking carefully about the future. Remember, all decisions have an element of fantasy and speculation because you must imagine the future. If you will be implementing your decision soon, you probably can anticipate the upcoming circumstances reasonably well. Predicting the distant future, however, is difficult. Even so, there are patterns of events and behaviors that you can use as references to "guesstimate" circumstances that might exist when your decisions will be implemented. Law libraries, business case studies, technical journals, biographies, and government records are a few well-known sources of helpful history. For more personal decisions, you might wish to consult family, friends, and teachers/professors for their knowledge, experience, and input. The most difficult decisions are those for which no precedent exists or can be found, such as being willing to be the first person to break the sound barrier. Other difficult decisions are those that must be made quickly, with little background information. As much as possible, thoughtful processes should accompany all decisions, whether ordinary or extraordinary. Your choices give you a chance to arrange your future according to your desires. With each decision, something else occurs. What you choose to do becomes an expression of who you are—giving you a defining character imprint that you will share with family, friends, and colleagues.

Implementing Your Decision

However, just making a decision is as useless as having an uncracked nut. You have to open it to the world by implementing your decision. Set up an action agenda—what must be done by whom, when, where, why, with what, and how. If you do this right away, you will have better command of your purposes and needs, and the problem is least likely to change before you have a chance to solve it. Flow charts and tree diagrams can be useful. Make sure to include an evaluation or some signal of success into your action agenda so you will know whether you have chosen wisely.

Also, periodically review your decision. A good modern example is the existence of "Sunset Laws" 📖 . Few decisions are irreversible; in almost all situations change, retrofit ↩, or new accommodations are possible. There are two cautions. The first is to avoid foolish vacillation ↩. Once you make a decision, live with it at least long enough to allow time to prove its worth or worthlessness. The second is to treat yourself kindly. If you decided honestly on the basis of the possible evidence and thought, then your decision was the right one—even if it turned out badly. If the results were fantastic, allow yourself a small helping of BLT (the celebrity sandwich known as Bright Lights and Trumpets) and go on as before. Then, get ready for your next decision making challenge, all the while remembering that decisions are like bread—common, nourishing, and often full of holes.

You might like to try some of the ideas in this chapter by working on a current problem of interest to you. Your progress could be recorded in the blank pages that follow, or in your personal notebook.

Summary

☞ Your background—including your personality, knowledge base, cultural and personal experiences, values, and interests—affect your decision making processes.

☞ Problems often have more than one right answer.

☞ Avoiding making a decision is itself a decision and can result in an unfavorable outcome.

☞ Good decisions can be reached by following one or more procedures.

☞ A listing of pros and cons can be a quick aid in making choices.

☞ An in-depth process of decision making involves a five-stage method.

☞ Decisions need to be followed by action, usually promptly.

☞ Periodically review and evaluate your decisions.

The strongest principle of growth lies in human choice.

– George Eliot

Decision is a risk rooted in the courage of being free.

– Paul Tillich

Don't fight the problem; decide it.
– General George C. Marshall

It is a common experience that a problem difficult at night is resolved in the morning after the committee of sleep has worked on it.
– John Steinbeck

Decision is a sharp knife that cuts clean and straight. Indecision is a dull one that hacks and tears and leaves ragged edges behind.
– Jan McKeithen

We have freedom of choice, yes, but not freedom from choice.

– Mary Ellen Edwards

Your Ideas

_____

_____

_____

_____

_____

_____

_____

_____

_____

_____

_____

_____

_____

_____

_____

_____

_____

_____

_____

_____

_____

_____

I have accepted fear as a part of life—specifically the fear of change.... I have gone ahead despite the pounding in the heart that says: turn back ....   — **Erica Jong**

Your Ideas

_____

_____

_____

_____

_____

_____

_____

_____

_____

_____

_____

_____

_____

_____

_____

_____

_____

_____

_____

_____

_____

He will not dither. He will decide. He will not agonize; he will act.
– Hubert H. Humphrey

Chapter 8
Frustration

Mr. S is normally a pleasant person; that's how he got his nickname—Mr. S for Mr. Smile. But right now he seems to be a miserable grouch as he harshly criticizes what you consider to be your best work. You try to contain both your anger and a sick feeling, mumbling words like *I guess so; probably; but I tried* that have no effect upon his continuing tirade ᨀ. Before long, you mentally slip away into a private reverie ᨀ, an imaginative response as a coping mechanism to your predicament.

You picture yourself crawling down a long corridor with a three-foot ceiling and one door at the end. You don't even know if the door is locked. Then you discover that the door at the end is just an illusion—a mirror or a surrealistic ᨀ painting. The corridor turns and there is almost no light.

You ask yourself some questions: "Why am I doing this? Who cares? Why wasn't I warned? I should have been given the proper tools. This task is impossible. But if I don't succeed, what will they think of me? Who will talk to me? Should I backtrack while I still have some sense of where I came from?"

With your head pounding and body totally stressed, the anger rises. The space is too small to hold you. The dispassionate ᨀ

walls will not respond to flailing arms. But then you take a deep breath and stop to consider your dilemma. You think that maybe Mr. S is having a bad day because something has happened to him. Maybe tomorrow he will reconsider his reaction to your work.

This imagery describes how we often feel when we are in a frustrating situation—trapped, powerless, self-critical, and angry. The reaction to frustration is physical as well as mental. Many people, including health professionals, believe that high stress levels can result in the accumulation of harmful chemicals in the body, which in turn may lead to migraine headaches, ulcers, heart attacks, high blood pressure, arthritis, and vision problems. Fatigue, exhaustion, and mental or physical breakdowns are possible. Surprisingly, such physical consequences are not the result of intense and stressful activity when it accompanies successful venture. The metabolic ⚭ debris forms chemical "scars" only as a result of the stress when it leads to failure—either real or imagined.

Does this mean that you should become so emotionally detached from your environment that nothing ever bothers you? No, but you can learn how to minimize stress, handle it, and turn it to your advantage.

Stress Is a Double Edged Sword

There are times when stress is a good thing. When getting ready to give a speech or other performance in front of an audience, stress can actually bring your efforts to a sharp focus and make your performance better than it would have been without a few "nerves." Stress can also alert you to danger and make your reflexes sharper as, for example, when you are outdoors in heavy snow or a rainstorm. Stress can be beneficial because it can bring a focus to your abilities to handle problems or alert you to danger.

Stress is harmful only when you inwardly "gnaw" on it without a creative outlet or a constructive attitude. Knowing what to do when you become frustrated and overloaded by stress can improve your chances of living longer with better health.

Perhaps more immediately debilitating ⚭ than various physical reactions to stress are the emotional consequences of continued frustration. Unless you learn to manage frustration adequately, the resulting unhappiness, anger, and self-hate you may feel can render you incapable of reacting sensibly. You may even think about suicide. You are not a bad person if you have ever had suicidal thoughts. Many people have had such thoughts, but wisely have not acted upon them. Thinking about suicide can be a reaction to what seems—at the time—to be an impossible situation. You may need to realize that virtually all problems are of short duration (at least in their real effect upon you) as long as you are alive. Therefore, thinking about ending your life could be a normal passing thought when you are in a tough, but temporary, situation; but acting upon this impulse is not normal and certainly not desirable. If you have gone so far as to think how you would "do it," you should get help. Help is as near as your phone. Many communities have people who are available to answer telephone calls on a 24-hour basis to provide appropriate counseling. Check the front of your telephone book for this number—usually listed as *Crisis and Suicide Counseling*. The people at these crisis lines have been specially trained to handle calls like this.

Otherwise, talk to someone you trust. Be honest and listen carefully. Suicide has long-lasting and far reaching implications for many different people who have been associated with you. It leaves a wound that never heals for the survivors; this wound is more painful than that left by accidental death or death from an illness. Years later, people may still be hurt because of your choice. Your brothers or sisters may resent that you didn't stick around so that their children could know you. Parents will grieve that you left the world before you had discovered your true gift or passion. And while some suicides are done to hurt or "get back at" someone else, as in "I'll show them," the person most hurt of course is the one who kills himself.

As an alternative to this irrevocable act that will affect so many lives besides your own, think of ways to use your considerable talents to help others have a better life. Even if you feel you have no control over a particular situation, you can learn to manage your viewpoint or attitude about that situation, or you can make a plan to get out of the situation eventually.

Another undesirable coping mechanism for a frustrating situation is to regress to early childhood and act like a baby. You are too grown up to do this, but among your acquaintances, there may be some "old babies." Typical behaviors of these immature adults include temper tantrums, throwing things, being unreasonably silly, avoiding or ignoring the cause or circumstance of the problem, or pretending not to be frustrated.

Here is one example of possible childish reactions to a problem. Consider that you have lost or mislaid expensive tickets to a concert that you and a friend have looked forward to for a long time. You have forgotten that the tickets are where you put them—in a safe place, under a lamp on your desk. In your frustration, you accuse others of losing them, or you scream at the dog who is begging for dinner while you are searching. You could have a desperate "toss on the floor" search of your clothing, or you could avoid reality and delay calling your friend until it's too late and she shows up at the door. Then, to cover yourself, you invent a wild story.

In a perfect world, this situation wouldn't happen. Why? Because you would quickly find the tickets, or—even better—you would have such orderly habits that you would always know where your tickets are kept. But this is not a perfect world. Absolutes are rare; alternatives are common. It is helpful to remember that there is almost always more than one solution to any problem. Keeping this in mind can help relieve many otherwise stressful situations. When you don't find the tickets, you call your friend, and you rearrange the evening to do something else—a bit less enjoyable, perhaps, but acceptable to both of you.

Another situation involving frustration is one that results from moving to a new town. Imagine that you have just moved to Centerville. In your old town, you were well known, had many friends, and found it easy to get around by yourself in your wheelchair. Now, stairs and narrow doorways in most of these old buildings are daily sources of stress. Most frustrating of all, however, is the loneliness. Yet when old friends call, you make believe life is beautiful. In fact, though, you are really avoiding places and people and only pretending that you have an active social life. Then you discover that e-mail correspondence can be a daily source of joy, and in fact, you organize a chat room. Your difficulty in traveling to inhospitable places now seems less of a frustration. You have found a substitute and reduced the frustration—at least temporarily. Having nearby friends and freedom of movement are still important, but you have found a way to cope with the situation and accept what is, at present, possible. Doing this has required a positive attitude and simplification of desires on your part—both requiring self-discipline and positive ways to deal with stress and frustration.

A catalog of the likely sources of frustration would encompass every known experience—problems with material goods, processes, events, and human relationships. Every change—even vacations—involves coping, and thus stress. Natural events such as storms can trigger frustrations. Not doing something right or in a timely manner can be irritating. Although the catalog of possible frustrations is incredibly large, your personal attitude and approach to situations will determine whether or not problems will annoy or baffle you. And remember, someone else may consider the same situations to be challenging, humorous, or unimportant.

Losing, forgetting, or breaking things are common troublesome experiences and are frustrating. Like having accidents, these things may occur more frequently if you are mentally preoccupied. Chronic ♋ problems with any of these may be a symptom of other difficulties, and you should try to figure out why they occur (professional help may be advisable). To avoid memory problems, you may find it helpful to make lists of important information in your personal notebook, use computer stored data, and learn memory aids.

Ironically ♋, your most stressful experiences may actually be related to your strengths, particularly your creative interests and abilities. Stress might come from:

- Lack of opportunity to use your ability or talent.
- Insufficient access to an education appropriate to your talents and abilities.
- Rejection of your ideas by experts in your field or by a respected teacher.
- Insufficient opportunities to share your abilities with peers or in public settings.
- Personal fear of failure and/or public rejection of your ideas.

- Misappropriation ↷ by others of your ideas or creative works.
- Family, social, or cultural constraints—*You can't become a singer because we are a family of lawyers, judges, etc.*—or financial—*There isn't enough money.*
- Prejudice of any kind that limits your activity.
- Inability to find someone to help.
- Lack of materials, instruments, or working space.
- Tackling some project too large for your present circumstances.
- Failure of health—mental or physical.
- Having so many interests that focus on any one of them is difficult.
- Failing badly in one endeavor and being unable to decide on a future direction. (Remember, failure is just the discovery of what doesn't work. What will work still exists and is possible.)
- Dealing socially with people who think you are "weird" because of your creativity or beliefs.

Coping with Frustration

All these frustrations may seem overwhelming, but they needn't be. The following table lists some possible frustrating attitudes and their "antidotes" ↷. Can you relate these suggestions to any of your previous experiences? Would looking at problems in this way have been helpful? You might like to record some of your reactions in your personal notebook or at the end of this chapter.

Attitudes That Can Lead To Frustration	Attitudes That Tend To Decrease Frustration
I can't do anything about this. I'm blocked because:	*I can handle this because:*
1. I'm powerless.	1. I can find an alternative, obtain help, be patient, or look forward to a day when I will have power. I can learn about how people use or misuse power.
2. No one understands me. No one cares about me.	2. I appreciate being *alive*—and being able to survive to this point. I am worth a lot just for surviving. I do not expect myself to be perfect or a master of every situation. What counts is that I care about myself. There are things that I can do for myself. I'm going to try to be the best there is at x (where x is anything you undertake), because it could be a worthwhile experience.
3. This routine is killing me. It's dull and boring. Sometimes there is too much pressure.	3. I have not made a lifetime commitment to this. I can add something or do something else that gives me some satisfaction, or a sense of achievement, even if I have to keep *this* routine for now.

Attitudes That Can Lead To Frustration	Attitudes That Tend To Decrease Frustration
I can't do anything about this. I'm blocked because:	*I can handle this because:*
4. I can't seem to get anything right. I seem to mess up every time.	4. I have confidence in myself. I'll do my best, then let it go if it's impossible. In any case, I'll know more about myself and be more able in the future.
	My happiness does not depend on someone else's opinion of me, so I don't have to worry about failure.
	I can ask someone for advice, feedback, or evaluation.
5. I wish I could do this, but I don't know how.	5. I can proceed carefully. I've got a chance to do something unusual. Maybe it is risky, and I may not know enough now, but it is a good opportunity to learn and contribute.
6. I can't get what I need or want.	6. Is it really that important? Is there an alternative? Do I really need or want it? Do I have to have it now? Maybe if I am patient, something better will turn up.

Attitudes That Can Lead To Frustration	Attitudes That Tend To Decrease Frustration
I can't do anything about this. I'm blocked because:	*I can handle this because:*
7. I can't decide.	7. I would rather make the choice than have someone make it for me. I can find whatever advice or information I need, list the pros and cons, take my time, look at alternatives, and think it through. Whatever decision I make will be the best one possible under these circumstances.
8. I'm too shy or <u>x</u>, (x equals anything else I use as an excuse).	8. This is important to me, and I am going to do it. I know it will be tough, but I can try. I'll take one step at a time. If all else fails, I'll try to get someone else to help.
9. No one has ever been in this situation before.	9. Even though this is a unique problem, I know I can find some way to tackle it. Maybe this is a good time to brainstorm possible solutions. I can also get some peaceful rest, observe nature, then approach this problem again. If I need help, I can get it.

Attitudes That Can Lead To Frustration	Attitudes That Tend To Decrease Frustration
I can't do anything about this. I'm blocked because:	*I can handle this because:*
10. It is too late. It is hopeless.	10. Even if it is too late this time, I will be better prepared next time. What else can I do? I can do something constructive with what time I have. I can try to make amends for any results of my inaction, perhaps by doing something on a smaller scale.

By now, you see the pattern. Solving stressful situations requires more than positive thinking, though that is important to most people. Think of that previously described imaginary move you made to Centerville when you were confined to a wheelchair and felt so alone. The positive attitudes in the preceding checklists (especially numbers 2, 5, 7, and 8) probably were helpful. Each problem requires developing definite techniques that are especially suited to your particular abilities, skills, and personality. These "schemes" or insights will help you solve recurrent problems. Experience helps you to accumulate more of these successful patterns, and the feelings of frustration will tend to diminish ↶ as you grow older and wiser. You are your own best investment. In perfecting yourself—your only real lifetime asset—you gain strength to meet adversity.

Remember that assistance will be needed for especially crushing situations. The best helper is a really close friend or family member. The next best helper is a "paper" friend (or two or three), such as a personally selected book of humor, poetry, or inspiration. Another valuable salve ↶ for frustration is physical exercise. This can be a brisk walk, a workout at a gym, or some physically challenging sport that you normally enjoy—such as tennis or swimming. Accumulate some of these resources, and use them when you are sorely stressed.

Purpose, more than anything else, cures the affliction of constant frustration. By seeing that you can give of yourself, produce in accord with your best insights, and create as truly as your inner visions permit, your capabilities are aroused and aimed fruitfully. You do not waste your strength and time in trivial, superficial ω, or petty dealings. You have prioritized your efforts.

Although it would be naive to think that all obstacles can be overcome, it is equally naive to think such obstacles will necessarily extinguish a passionate desire to achieve. Your ability to accomplish is not in question—ever. This comforting, and challenging, idea can keep you motivated during times of frustration. Remember that after becoming deaf, Beethoven wrote incredibly beautiful music. His passion still burned even in the face of incredible frustrations.

A powerful short story by Jean Giono, called *The Man Who Planted Trees*, chronicles the amazing efforts of one man to change his world. Originally published in *Vogue* magazine in 1954 as "The Man Who Planted Hope and Grew Happiness," it has become a classic. The listing in the bibliography at the end of this book is of an edition that is beautifully illustrated with wood engravings. Reading it may give you both pleasure and courage.

When your inner direction is steady and reliable, you can decide how best to negotiate any confining corridor of frustration. If your inner strength is based on carefully developed morals and ethics, you will have an excellent compass for daily living. A lifetime goal, which may evolve as you develop, will help you accomplish despite the obstacles of daily effort. From a purposeful sense of direction, you will derive energy and determination to succeed, a greatness of spirit, and a holding fast to goodness.

In the blank pages at the end of this chapter or in your notebook, list one or two of the most irritating frustrations that currently affect an important goal of yours. Occasionally review the problem, and note any possible solutions. Also note your response to the ideas in this chapter that seem particularly influential or interesting to you.

☞   Almost anything can be frustrating.

☞   Frustration can affect your mental and physical health.

☞   Your attitude and knowledge of useful techniques can help you manage troublesome situations.

☞   Friends can be valuable; "book friends" extend your source of help.

☞   Unclear, poorly defined, or unwise goals make frustration inevitable.

☞   By being true to yourself and your capacity for contribution, you can convert possible frustrations into opportunities.

The greater part of our happiness or misery depends on our disposition and not on our circumstances.

– Martha Washington

You may be disappointed if you fail, but you are doomed if you don't try.

– Beverly Sills

Post-mortems on defeats are never very useful unless they say something about the future.

– James Reston

When I am hassled about something, I always stop and ask myself what difference it will make in the evolution of the human species in the next ten million years, and that question always helps me to get back my perspective.

– Anne Wilson Schaef

We have to learn to be our own best friends because we fall too easily into the trap of being our own worst enemies.

– Roderick Thorp

Being defeated is often a temporary condition. Giving up is what makes it permanent.

– Marilyn vos Savant

Your Ideas

_____

_____

_____

_____

_____

_____

_____

_____

_____

_____

_____

_____

_____

_____

_____

_____

_____

_____

_____

One never notices what has been done; one can only see what remains to be done. **– Marie Curie**

Your Ideas

What I must do is all that concerns me, not what the people think.
– Ralph Waldo Emerson

> *A word is not a crystal, transparent and unchanging. It is the skin of a living thought and may vary greatly in color and content according to the circumstances and time in which it is used.*
> **– Justice Oliver Wendell Holmes**

Chapter 9
Brevity
and
Levity

Playing with words is a honing ⌒ process for creative thinking. The main purpose of this chapter is for you to have fun while briefly exploring a word game that promotes mental flexibility. This pleasant diversion of creativity—the levity of "fooling around"—sometimes results in a worthwhile new idea. But it will be worthwhile even if the only result is your inner sense of satisfaction and enjoyment in having solved a puzzle of no great consequence. Many highly creative people have an excellent internal "laugh button" which they use to generate imaginative associations, as well as to maintain a sense of perspective about their world. These people also cultivate opportunities to use their sense of humor when playing games.

The passage quoted below, *Two Unusual Words*, is based on a recording of an actual mental ramble through stored ideas and impressions. (It is not quite the equivalent of a Virginia Woolf "recording" as in *Mrs. Dalloway* 📖, but it is similar.) It is an illustration of the linking of ideas to one another based on personal knowledge and experience. Everything in this collection of words had personal meaning to the author—and possibly not much significance (as a whole) to anyone else. But to create connections from one phrase to another will require you to flexibly use analytical thought and knowledge, and you may find this to be an interesting challenge.

Read *Two Unusual Words* initially without making any serious effort at comprehension. Then continue on and examine *The Cascade Word Game,* and then try a few of your own idea sequences. Afterwards, you might come back and enjoy a rereading of *Two Unusual Words*.

Two Unusual Words

*Brevity and levity are unusual words; they have similar shapes, sounds, and sizes. Is there a verbal connection, a meaning shared? "Brevity is the soul of **wit**." What is wit? A **wit** is an imaginatively perceptive and articulate individual especially skilled in banter or **persiflage**. **Persiflage**, with a Latin origin meaning hiss, corresponds to **frivolous** or lightly derisive talk or manner of treating a subject. Excessive or unseemly **frivolity** corresponds to **levity**. **Levity** also is the opposite of **gravity**, where **gravity** carries the sense of being weighty or **ponderous**. Then **ponderous** has as synonyms bulky, massive, **huge**, unwieldy, and cumbersome. **Huge** has **small** as an antonym. **Small** can be a synonym for **short**. One of the synonyms for **brevity** is **shortness**. There is a connection! If you think that this hiss has the sibilant sound of a goose, you are mistaken. It is not a wild goose chase even though **sibilare** is Latin for **hiss**.*

*Another turn to take begins with brevity. Digging to the heart of a problem. The briefest way of describing. The least time possible on mundane chores equals an explosion of fun time. Time to **organize** a mental riot by linking ideas to produce a valuable entity. Weeks to produce a ten-word advertising slogan; minutes to write a one-page letter. Personal shorthand. Pruned fruit trees. Satire has a Latin origin (**satura**) meaning a dish filled with various fruit. The order-*

*ing of pamplemousse in a Parisian restaurant. (It is not a better variety of chocolate mousse.) Fruit trees—pleached. Word linkage—a mental web. Geese. Feet. The nature of thought processes. Less is more. More is not enough. Sir Thomas More. Becket. T.S. Eliot. **The Wasteland**.*

*Time for something else. Levity. Levitation. A balloon ride over the French countryside. Balloon vine. Cardiospermum halicacabum. A sapindaceous tropical climbing plant. Cardio? Heart. Balloon? Halicacabum! Bum! Sapindaceous. Sap! Light humor. What is ridiculous? Why? Why is laughter contagious? Is laughter essential? Why? Passage from wit to levity. A balloon ride—up, over, and down. The English downs. Sheep. **All Things Bright and Beautiful**. Beautiful laughter. Laughter in the place of anger. Laughter to preserve sanity. A cleanser. Abrasive. Polish. A polished speech. The introductory joke. **The Modern Handbook of Humor**. Dr. George Harris, addressing an assembly at Amherst College: "I intended to give you some advice, but now I remember how much is left over from last year unused." The place of honor in a procession is at the end. Rosebuds. Robert Herrick. The quest ends demonstrative. Stop.*

The playfulness inherent ✍ in the idea sequence of *Two Unusual Words* can be achieved almost anywhere, anytime. No equipment is needed except you—no game board, no racquet, no special shoes. A mind teeming ✍ with ideas, memories, recallable sights, facts, and words, is all that is necessary. Playing this mental game involves a cascade ✍ of your thoughts, starting either with a word which is of personal interest or a word selected randomly (perhaps from a book, selection of photographs, fabric swatch book, tool catalog, seed list, etc.).

Consider the following word sequences as examples of the *Cascade Word Game*. They are brief digressions ✍ involving word associations. They start with the first word and, by simple association, come to the word below it and so forth, until the process reaches a creative end. The search for the next word involves you thinking of, and then discarding, ideas that are not personally suitable until something finally "clicks" and you find a word you like.

Cascade Word Game

This mind-stretching game can be played easily in brief moments of solitude. Unlike the nearly constant and often rambling internal mental chatter going on in our minds, this thinking is more organized and deliberate. With this, like all games, some results are better than others. Try aiming at occasional silliness and verbal slapstick *&^*. Think of it as a mental romp *&^*. Like jazz, it is disciplined and yet creative. Explore the *Cascade Word Game* often, perhaps as a way to make standing in line somewhere more interesting. Record some of your best efforts in this book or in your personal notebook.

Example 1

Brevity
Brief
Leif
Lief
Laugh
Cry

In this first example, a near synonym of *brevity* begins the cascade with the word *brief.* The ending sound brief, brought *Leif* (of Leif Ericson, Viking explorer 📖) to mind, and this was bounced to *lief* (which means gladly, willingly), which led to *laugh* and then its sensory antonym, *cry.*

Example 2

Levity
Lever
Ever
Ere
Verity
Very

In this second example, a quick response to *levity* was *lever*, because of the similar verbal beginning. Then the word *ever* was an easy choice since it was enclosed in *lever*. A bit of mental maneuvering produced *ere* (meaning before). Then the easy process ended. *Ere* produced no immediate response. A mental shuffling of shapes, sounds, and meanings occurred with a scanning of all of the preceding words. *Verity* (meaning truth) popped up next. Searching backwards, *ever* yielded *ver*. A visual alignment with the shape and size of *levity* led to *verity*. Quickly, *very* formed as a final word out of both ends of *verity*.

The *Cascade Word Game* is a playful, but disciplined, way to explore relationships within your personal knowledge bank. Although these two examples of word cascades were developed using the key chapter words, *brevity* and *levity*, any other set of words or terms could have been used. There is no intent to make these mental chains enhance only the meaning of *brevity* and *levity*. The purpose is to trigger mental searching processes; partly conscious, partly unconscious; partly emotional, partly analytical.

There are three word games in this book, each of increasing complexity. In *Chapter 4: Creative Thought Processes*, a linkage between two given terms is sought. In the present chapter, one term is the progenitor ᴇᴏ for a series of related terms. This may be slightly more difficult because of the greater degree of freedom in approaching a "solution" to the game. The last game in *Chapter 23: All of Your Tomorrows* is best played when you have completed this book.

Finally, the terms *brevity* and *levity* may encourage you to think about the nature of discovery. Kary Mullis 📖, a Nobel Laureate in chemistry, refers to this process of investigation as follows: "Simplicity is embarrassing when you have to work for months to achieve it.… You ... will wonder why people get the Nobel Prize for pointing out such simple things. The answer is that most people can't see the simple things and the simple things are always the most important." In this sense, the brevity (or simplicity) of $f=ma$ or $E=mc^2$ corresponds to heroic thinking about the nature of the universe. Perhaps the *Cascade Word Game* will help you in discovering the important simple things in life and how to do so with levity.

Summary

☞ The briefest and best possible statement often requires the most intense examination of many ideas.

☞ The most elegant theorems create order out of considerable chaos—as in $E=mc^2$.

☞ Your ability to create order depends upon the amount of disorder that you can comfortably store and eventually rearrange.

☞ Accumulate ideas like a pack rat; try using ideas in the Cascade Word Game instead of single words.

☞ Use levity as a pry bar to stir up your mental collection of data.

☞ Enjoy each day.

W**o**rds of W**i**sd**o**m

As long as one keeps searching, the answers come.

– Joan Baez

[It was] an initiation into the love of learning, of learning how to learn, that was revealed to me by my BLS masters as a matter of interdisciplinary cognition—that is, learning to know something by the relation to something else.

– Leonard Bernstein

Life forms illogical patterns. It is haphazard and full of beauties which I try to catch as they fly by, for who knows whether any of them will ever return?

– Margot Fonteyn

The clouds gathered together, stood still and watched the river scuttle around the forest floor, crash headlong into haunches of hills with no notion of where it was going, until exhausted, ill and grieving, it slowed to a stop just twenty leagues short of the sea.

– Toni Morrison

No day in which you learn something is a complete loss.

– David Eddings

I never learn anything talking. I only learn when I ask questions.

– Lou Holtz

Your Ideas

The test of a first-rate intelligence is the ability to hold two opposed ideas in the mind at the same time, and still retain the ability to function. **– F. Scott Fitzgerald**

Your Ideas

Piling up knowledge is as bad as piling up money. You have to begin sometime to kick around what you know.   **– Robert Frost**

Chapter 10
Self-Esteem

Although self-esteem fluctuates, you are never without it. It is your psychological barometer ᷧ, responding to the pressures of daily life much as your outer skin responds to physical pressure. Just as a healthy outer skin is a desirable entity, so too is a healthy inner self-esteem. With it, even miserable days can be valuable.

On some days, you find both shoes, walk out into a beautiful sunny morning, say exactly the right things to someone, and hear exactly what you wish to hear in return. You smile going to sleep. On other days, the shoes still fit, but nothing else does. Your reactions to the good and the bad, the expected and unexpected, your moods and the moods of others—all of these contribute to your "inner self" and your self-esteem.

So, how do you develop a healthy self-esteem? You accept the fact that truly doing your best each day provides the real definition of your success. Your best may not correspond to someone else's standard of perfection, but it doesn't have to. Remember that perfectionism is by definition illogical. Omniscience ᷧ and infallibility ᷧ are not attainable human characteristics.

However, truly doing your best each day in matters that are important can be a real challenge that requires honesty and effort. Honesty dictates that you make efforts consistent with everything that you know about yourself and your surroundings. Effort involves striving for effectiveness in your immediate daily activities, as well as a consciously planned preparation for the future. Preparation for the future implies not only a projected image of yourself in that future, but also an awareness of what might be required for you to arrive at that future state.

The preceding simple sentence describes an enormous complexity—sufficient to occupy your attention for the rest of your life. One complication is that you must know yourself. Events in childhood, and afterward, help shape your perception of yourself. That perception can be warped. For example, if you were an over-protected child and kept from situations in which you would have to make decisions, you may not currently respect your own judgment capabilities. That doesn't mean that you cannot choose wisely, it only means that you may have to develop this skill by trial and error now, since you did not have opportunities to do so earlier.

If you grew up in a constantly critical atmosphere, you may believe that anything less than perfection is just not good enough. Since you have accepted external, perfectionistic standards that are unrealistic, you may try to do very little. As a result, you may feel worthless. However, by making a determined effort to refute *&* this burden of perfectionism, you *can* function very capably. Although a message such as "needs better organization" on a paper or report may convey a lack of worth to you, it may not have been intended that way. Some comments you take very personally may have been intended simply as helpful constructive criticism.

When you hear yourself thinking: "I'm always wrong," "I failed; what's the use in trying," "If only I'd had the sense to…", **STOP**. Flip the tape over and hear instead: "I've been right many times before. This mistake teaches me that there is a different answer from the one I chose. I'll remember the right answer for this occasion. This mistake doesn't erase all of my previous successes, nor does it foretell future failures. I've just got some more learning to do."

You need to realize your own worthiness—that you are a good person with a unique set of talents and abilities. *Everyone* is special, *everyone* can enjoy each day, and *everyone* can add something to the total sum of human experience. You must absorb this idea deeply into yourself—your "inner skin" has to accept the impression that you are okay. And remember that feeling "okay" has to be cultivated.

Elements of Self-Esteem

Self-esteem is a combination of self-confidence and self-respect. Self-confidence develops from repeated successful experiences in handling events, in interacting with people, and in making good daily choices. Self-respect depends on being honorable in your daily actions, in accord with principles or standards that you have accepted and developed for your personal use.

Consider, as an example, the choices made by a very successful musician who "reworked" material developed by lesser-known contemporaries. The recognition that he receives contributes to his self-confidence in stage appearances. He may believe that his creativity is honorable—that he has a legitimate reason to build upon the ideas of others. In this case, his self-respect is well founded, as is his self-esteem. But suppose he knows that his success is dishonorable, based on his fraudulent efforts to claim undeserved originality. If this bothers him, his self-respect and self-esteem will suffer despite his success. Although there are universal standards of behavior, it is the individual's awareness and acceptance of these standards that determine his regard for himself.

Now consider a not-so-successful musician who confidently continues to work hard despite limited recognition. If he has faith in his ability, he continues to write music and has high self-esteem. But if he knowingly makes minimal efforts to produce original compositions, his sense of self-worth diminishes, and he may need to re-examine his choice of occupation.

The way in which these two musicians react to criticism probably varies. As self-esteem plunges, over-reaction and defensive responses to criticism tend to rise. In contrast, a confident person can see criticism as a potentially useful information source.

Some situations will require you to give extra attention and care to issues of self-esteem. You might be an innovator, an explorer, or someone working at the interface of the new and the old. Other people may view your wonderful discoveries as bizarre, unimportant, and useless. But if you believe in your efforts and their value, your self-esteem is less likely to crumple.

If you can do many things with better-than-average ease, you may attempt more than is practical, and you may end up over-worked or feeling used. Other people may take advantage of your abilities by offering you many special tasks that will take "only a few minutes." Learn how to be selective so that you can do justice to whatever you undertake. If you tackle too much and just achieve mediocrity ᧠, your self-esteem may suffer.

When you excel at something, take care that you do not become so absorbed that you forget to respond to the efforts of others or recognize the contributions of others in that area. It is possible to focus on a task so exclusively that you may become "vacuum packed"—that is, nearly totally self-contained and unresponsive to outside influences. This self-absorption may simply come from a fascination with the projects at hand. But sometimes a focus on achievements can actually be a form of trophy hunting and a need for approval—a symptom of low self-esteem.

All of us experience times when we feel disappointed in our efforts or when our efforts are not valued or appreciated by others. Sometimes we may even be strongly criticized. This can cause us to change our self-perceived status from high to low. What happens then to your level of self-esteem? *It need not and should not decrease.* Although we should be open to evaluation from others or from within ourselves, this doesn't need to drastically influence our self-esteem. Self-esteem is self-described and self-contained. You are yourself—you do not increase or decrease in ability because of the opinions of others. You should listen to these opinions but validate yourself on the basis of an inner integrity ᧠. Value the importance of achieving rather than the competitiveness that may lead to achievement.

Finally, you may fear that if you depend on others, it is an indication of weakness or low self-esteem. But remember, no one is omniscient, infallible, or completely self-reliant. By sharing abilities, insights and efforts, the sum becomes greater than its parts. You have much to offer. Others do also.

Maintaining and Improving Self-Esteem

The following is a list of some of the things that you can do to maintain and improve your self-esteem. Try any that interest you.

• Keep a scrapbook, picture album, or personal notebook to record achievement and point toward future possibilities.

• Develop a hobby or recreational interest that you can turn to when other occupations become troublesome.

• Practice giving deserved compliments to others. As you perceive the good in others, so too will you be more sensitive to your own goodness.

• Regard failures as learning experiences. You will learn what you *can* do—not just what you cannot do.

• If all things that you do are easy, then you need to move to areas that are *not* so easy. Unless you stretch yourself, how else will you really find out what you can do?

• *Plan* to enjoy something each day. Respond to something pleasurable to revive your spirit.

• Make an inventory of your assets. Look at them occasionally. What can you do very well? What have you accomplished?

• Work at self-improvement. Consider what you can do to overcome handicaps; compensate for weaknesses. Set goals, and develop a plan of action. Decide to do something by a certain date; put it on your personal calendar.

- Associate with optimistic ⅋ people.
- Read literature, including time-proven works of art that can extend your awareness of "the human condition."
- Picture yourself as being what you want to be, what you believe is the real you. Do this as a mental exercise before undertaking any serious task.
- Surround yourself with positive suggestions. Plant sayings, proverbs, catch phrases, or personal exhortations in your wallet, on a notebook, in your desk, on a mirror frame, or on the blank pages following this chapter.
- Regularly plan to give something, while expecting nothing in return. Giving will help you realize the vitality of your inner core and your accomplishments.
- Recognize that self-assertion is a non-aggressive act. It is a compassionate ⅋ revelation of self, a willingness to extend outward, to accept and share responsibilities. Join a group or association that will permit your active, assertive participation.
- Set up rewards for yourself. Do something special to celebrate accomplishments.
- Create a private salvage system for your days of low self-esteem. It may include talking to someone for reassurance, reading something humorous or inspirational, or spending time doing something that you really like to do and do well. Have this system established in advance of need, and make sure that it really adds to your well-being.

You might like to look at the following list and add any words that you deem appropriate:

Share, stimulate, succeed, subordination &, spiritual, see
Enjoy, express, ego
Love, link
Forgive, find, fear

Accept, accordance, advantage
Preserve, power, play
Patience, praise
Reason, respect, right, relinquish, relations, reveal
Organize, optimism
Value, virtues, vindicate &
Activate, abilities, art
Learn, live

Summary

☞   The desire for self-esteem is basic to life.

☞   A healthy self-esteem develops when you do your best each day.

☞   Your perception of reality affects how you regard yourself.

☞   You need to recognize and address problems that may arise because of your talented nature.

☞   Certain activities will enhance your acceptance of yourself.

Words of Wisdom

Don't compromise yourself. You are all you've got.

– Janis Joplin

I desire so to conduct the affairs of this administration that if at the end, when I come to lay down the reins of power, I have lost every other friend on earth, I shall at least have one friend left, and that friend shall be down inside of me.

– Abraham Lincoln

When we can begin to take our failures non-seriously, it means we are ceasing to be afraid of them. It is of immense importance to learn to laugh at ourselves.

– Katherine Mansfield

Nobody can make you feel inferior without your consent.

– Eleanor Roosevelt

Be yourself. No one can ever tell you're doing it wrong.

– James Leo Herlihly

Every time we start thinking we're the center of the universe, the universe turns around and says with a slightly distracted air, "I'm sorry. What'd you say your name was again?"

– Margaret Maron

Your Ideas

_____

_____

_____

_____

_____

_____

_____

_____

_____

_____

_____

_____

_____

_____

_____

_____

_____

_____

_____

_____

_____

_____

Love yourself first and everything else falls into line. You really have to love yourself to get anything done in this world.
– Lucille Ball

Your Ideas

_____

_____

_____

_____

_____

_____

_____

_____

_____

_____

_____

_____

_____

_____

_____

_____

_____

_____

_____

_____

Always be a first-rate version of yourself, instead of a second-rate version of somebody else. **– Judy Garland**

Chapter 11
Conversational Skills

Do you realize that those who succeed, who are promoted to important positions, or who are popular at social gatherings are often those who talk engagingly and distinctively? Others of equal potential are sometimes overlooked, not because they lack interesting ideas, but because they lack conversational skills.

As with any skill, practice is needed in the art of smooth and interesting conversation. Additionally, it is important to recognize that mental stability, perspective, and self-understanding often derive from daily contact with people; thus all human interactions are valuable. Even if you are very busy, include some social occasions in your schedule. Take advantage of conversational opportunities.

Here are some guidelines that may help you become a better conversationalist:

- Maintain appropriate body language, including looking at people and maintaining a reasonable amount of eye contact.

- Avoid all self-enclosing gestures, such as folded arms or hiding behind a book, and eschew &⁀noise-making movements such as chewing gum.
- Have a friendly face that is alert, obviously receptive, and smiling when appropriate.
- Stand before a mirror and practice "smiling" with your mouth closed. Your eye openings and facial appearance change; you *look* pleasant. When you look at someone that way, they will want to talk with you.

Of course, you don't want to talk all the time. Listening is a key part of any good conversation. And when you do talk, you don't want to be a bore. What good is all of your rich, internalized wisdom and knowledge if you often say trite &⁀, tiresome, or depressing things? Make use of the following guidelines on every possible occasion. As in most activities, thoughtful practice and self-awareness will help you succeed.

Don't Chatter or Talk Constantly

Let others have their chance. Find a subject of interest to the *other* person. This will diminish your self-consciousness, and will please the other person. It also gives you the best opportunity to learn something; thus, everyone wins.

Don't Be Chronically Silent

The perpetual listener is often thought of as being dull, uninterested, and/or unfriendly. When listening, look at the speaker, occasionally nod your head, or add a brief comment to show interest.

Select a Subject and Intelligently Pursue It

At tonight's dinner table, catch the first thought of general interest and direct it to someone. If you receive no response, ask a question. Try to stay with this topic as long as possible, perhaps thirty minutes. *Prolonged* examination of a topic changes superficial chitchat into valuable conversation.

Guide Conversation

Ask yourself: "Will anyone remember this conversation tomorrow?" If not, try to change the subject tactfully to something more useful or relevant. How? Use the "that reminds me of" technique. Even tiresome comments on weather can be deflected toward economics, science, art, or almost any other area if you are imaginative. Be *prepared* to effect such a change.

Consider the following exchange:

> *"It has been a really hot summer."*
> *"Do you think it is exceptional?"*
> *"As far as I am concerned, yes."*

Possible directing response:

> *"Does it make you believe in the Greenhouse Effect 📖?"*

Another possible technique is to ask advice *sincerely*. This is a great way to redirect a superficial ⌒ conversation.

> **X:** *"My dog is so smart that he knows just what I'm saying. He is almost human."*
>
> **You:** *"Oh, before I forget, should we set up that meeting with John?"*
>
> **X:** *"Well, next Saturday afternoon would be okay. As I was saying ...."*
>
> **You:** *"Do you think that John's idea is sensible? Can we get it done before December?"*

The net result is a conversation guided toward something mutually useful. Yet another way to change the subject or enliven a dying conversation is by using some item of scenery or circumstance to draw the speaker's attention to a new topic.

Be Considerate

When practical, you can welcome newcomers to a group conversation by mentioning their names; this may help encourage other members of the group (who may not know or remember the names of the new persons) to include them. Then try to help newcomers become aware of the current topic, perhaps by restating a key point from earlier in the conversation.

Develop Interesting Ideas

Your personal notebook can be a rich source of conversational gambits ☞. Reserve a section to record unusual facts, notable quotes, book titles, items related to your work, or items of interest to friends. Try to make one abbreviated entry per day for a month. Observe, read, or think of something *each* day that you consider exciting. You may wish to put some of your best entries in the blank pages at the end of this chapter.

One of the best ways to be prepared with interesting ideas for conversational topics is to read the local newspaper regularly. If time is short, scan headlines and lead paragraphs. Regularly read a few unusual magazines. Become familiar with current bestsellers, and read as many of these books as time and taste allow. Know something about your neighborhood—past or upcoming concerts, art exhibits, sports events, plays, and lectures. Watch television specials.

Psychological research suggests that as much as eighty percent of all of our conversation is trivial, aimless, and filled with cliches ☞! For instance, remarks about a television program in terms of cast, program length, and time of broadcast are often trivial. Talking about what the program meant to you or what kinds of questions it raised is more likely to be meaningful. For example, if a friend is interested in architecture, discussing a TV special on Frank Lloyd Wright 📖 could be mutually enjoyable and worthwhile.

With some thought, you can almost immediately discover one or more conversational subjects that interest people. Some helpful conversation openers could range from: "What did you do last weekend?" to "If you had an extra hundred dollars to spend tomorrow, what would you do?" Think up some similar openers suitable to your conversation circles.

Younger people generally like to discuss the present and the future; older people often like to discuss the past. Be prepared to give and take at each end of the time spectrum. The rich brocade ๛ of the past is best woven by those who lived in it, while the gauzy wings of the future fly wildly in young dreams. Instead of becoming impatient with narratives derived from the "good-old-days," encourage them. You will never have a better chance to learn that kind of history—intensely personalized. The events you read about in books become real when you listen to someone who actually was there. Likewise, when futuristic ideas irritate you because they seem too far-fetched, stir up your own imagination. Try to "top" them and you will probably end up having some real fun. You might enjoy reading *Global Trends 2005: An Owner's Manual for the Next Decade* by Michael J. Mazarr (1999). This book should give a year's supply of exciting conversational fuel.

Avoid Touchy Subjects

Try to avoid potentially argumentative subjects unless you are very well acquainted with the other person. Especially in group situations, avoid personal subjects such as weight, personal habits, or appearance that might hurt feelings or lead to gossip sessions. Religious beliefs, politics, or personal relationships may also be controversial ๛, and thus difficult subjects to discuss in certain situations.

Develop Vocabulary

Work at building an interesting word supply. Deliberately strike overworked words and terms from your speech, and teach yourself to use substitutes. Some common repetitive terms include "awesome," "okay," "like," "really," "no way," or "you know."

What you say in casual conversation with friends usually requires a slightly different vocabulary than what you use speaking in more formal occasions, such as an interview. However, in both cases, interesting and appropriate words will mark you as being someone special and worth listening to.

Alexander Hamilton 📖 once gave a speech in New York City that earned him a reputation as an intelligent politician and potential statesman. He was 17 years old. Fifteen years later in 1789, at age 32, he became the first United States Secretary of the Treasury.

Speeches and conversations show a sense of a person's character. Mr. Hamilton's use of language earned him the respect of his listeners. Your determination to learn new words and use them with precision and skill may likewise earn you the respect of *your* listeners.

Cultivate a Pleasant Voice

You may want to check your voice by recording it while reading something interesting. Experiment with changes in pitch and volume. Try to express emotion appropriately. Then listen to yourself. Consult library sources for remediation if you sound breathy, harsh, squeaky, or non-melodious. Breathing exercises can help. Listen carefully to how public speakers talk. Skilled speakers know how to change volume and pacing to maintain interest. Try doing this.

Control Diction

When listening to your voice recording, check for enunciation ✍. Can you understand each word? Are contracted words clear? Does "going to" sound like "gonna"? Pay attention to final d's and t's. Others often assess your cultural background by your speech. Sloppy speech may indicate, and indict ✍, a sloppy mind.

☞ Seek conversational opportunities.

☞ Adopt a receptive physical appearance.

☞ Be neither the monopolist nor the minimalist.

☞ Nurture an interesting subject to make it fruitful.

☞ Aim at making the conversation worthwhile.

☞ Be considerate; think of the other person.

☞ Prepare a richly furnished mind.

☞ Select topics wisely.

☞ Use the best possible tools: an appropriate vocabulary, a pleasant voice, and precise diction.

Words
of
Wisdom

Bore: a person who talks when you wish him to listen.   **– Ambrose Bierce**

The wit of conversation consists much less in showing a great deal of it than in bringing it out in others.

– La Bruyere

Television permits us to walk through life with minor speaking parts. And the more we fail to speak, the more difficult speaking becomes.   **– Lois Wyse**

Nothing lowers the level of conversation more than raising the voice.

– Stanley Horowitz

The true spirit of conversation consists in building on another man's observation, not overturning it.

– Edward G. Bulwer-Lytton

The real art of conversation is not to say the right thing in the right place, but to leave unsaid the wrong thing at the tempting moment.

– Dorothy Nevill

The value of the average conversation could be enormously improved by the constant use of four simple words: "I do not know."

– Andre Maurois

Your Ideas

_____

_____

_____

_____

_____

_____

_____

_____

_____

_____

_____

_____

_____

_____

_____

_____

_____

_____

_____

_____

_____

_____

Conversation means being able to disagree and still continue the discussion.
– Dwight MacDonald

Your Ideas

Silence may be as variously shaded as speech. **– Edith Wharton**

Chapter 12
Appearance

You come home late, slam the door, and fail to respond to a pleasant greeting. Or you come home late, have a tense look on your face, sit stiffly, and respond curtly ↩ to the greeting.

The two vignettes ↩ are so similar that, if you were acting in a play, it might take a skilled director to know which one of your portrayals interpreted a role more correctly.

You say that you are neither a director nor an actor. But you do represent (and present) yourself daily to others through your actions and appearance. How? Perhaps on a particular day something wonderful and extraordinary has occurred. But in response to the friendly question, "How are you doing?" you attempt to look nonchalant ↩ and hide your excitement, answering, "Oh, I'm okay." Your close friend will know that "something is up," however, because your actions are animated, and your eyes are bright. Your facial and body language have been more revealing than your words, and have given you away.

Appearance and actions are keys in communications between people. How can you improve your interactions with others? First, know yourself as you appear and choose to appear to others. Second, develop skill in reading faces and body language.

Learn To Read Faces and Body Language

There are many "dictionaries" for body language. Search out some of the modern references that exist in public libraries, especially those that are well illustrated. For example, *Eye to Eye, How People Interact*, by Peter Marsh (1988), provides useful pictures, and *Emotions, Journey Through the Mind and Body*, by the editors of Time Life Books (1994), has a few pages of photographs. When you visit an art gallery, look for subtleties ⚊ in the figures and faces of people portrayed by sensitive artists. Critically watching movies and television, possibly with the sound turned off, can increase your awareness of body language and its relationship to verbal language. Assess acting that is believable and observe people on various talk shows. Become more aware of the body movements of people that you meet and what those movements might convey.

Certain appearances are desirable in normal social situations because these patterns have commonly accepted meanings in our culture. For instance, frequently looking directly at someone when talking to them suggests honesty and interest in their reactions. Some body language is complex in its meaning. For example, a smile can sometimes be so brief that it is insincere, or it can be so long that it is a prolonged foolish grin. A sincere smile has a retention span that is just right. Try to observe this in people who are socially adept, and then practice your smile.

Evaluate Your Own Body Language

Evaluate the length of your walking stride, your posture, and the swinging of your arms. In conversations, notice your hand movements, eye opening, head angles, shrug styles, crossing of legs, manner of sitting, touching of hair or clothing, handling small objects, and folding of arms, plus innumerable combinations of those expressions that convey information about you. When you meet people for the first time, such as on interviews, you are judged initially by your appearance. There is an alert look that accompanies intelligence that is hard to fake, as opposed to a blank, vacuous ❧ stare. A vibrant, lively face, coupled with disciplined body movements, projects a desirable image and is charismatic ❧.

Surprisingly, your face can be shaped by choice—to some extent. By relaxing certain muscles, your lips look fuller and your face appears more "open." The narrowing of eyes or the raising of the forehead, when habitually practiced, produces a certain "set" to the face. Just as your handwriting changes as you mature, so too does your face in response to a maturing personality.

Be careful, however. What is considered to be good form in one social setting or culture may be offensive in another. In the Near East, people generally stand closer to each other than would be customary in other areas of the world. The private space of an individual is wider in the United States. Standing too close in the U.S. is an affront; standing too far away in the Near East is an insult or a sign of coldness. In some cultures, arm grabbing and hugging are an essential part of any greeting. In other cultures, this is offensive. You will become aware of these differences if you travel or interact within different cultural groups.

Body actions that tend to minimize below-the-neck attention are considered to be genteel ❧ evidence of social grace. Thus, large arm movements, sprawling body positions, and sexually suggestive motions are undesirable. There is logic to this. A sensitive person thinks that taking up more space than necessary is an imposition to be avoided. Also, any actions that increase facial attention will make sure that *verbal* communication is accurately received. Body language should enhance, even reinforce, the integrity of the spoken word as economically as possible. Repetitive body movements, such as obvious gum chewing, foot tapping, and hand swinging, are particularly irritating gestures to many people. Probably the best advice is to not chew gum in public—unless you can do so *very* discreetly.

Some of your distinctive gestures may be the result of unconscious mimicry ❧ of family members or friends. Try to be aware of what these mannerisms communicate to others. If they seem to

Outward Appearances Speak Loudly

irritate or offend others, practice until you delete them.

Spiky technicolor hair, partially shaved heads, very long locks, tattoos, and body piercings have all been used as statements to shock the "establishment" and to assert independence and convey individualism. At a minimum, a hairdo suggests the extent to which you are interested in yourself and your self-image. Hairstyles can be elaborate, distinctive, time-consuming, simple, contemporary, face framing, suitable, youthful, and all of the contrary descriptions. However, you are advertising yourself, and so your hairstyle, as well as the rest of your appearance, should be both comfortable and in keeping with your personality and how you want others to see you.

Clothing provides another medium for self-projection. What works for an artist such as Louise Nevelson 📖 or Salvador Dali 📖 would be unseemly for a politician or an engineer. Social expectation sets standards and limits for public dress. One of the most scientific dress code explicators ✍ is John P. Molloy 📖. His books are available in many libraries and may be of interest to you. What you choose to wear will change with the formality of a situation. Jeans worn for everyday are rarely suitable to be worn at interviews.

Make your daily grooming as complete as possible. An unkempt appearance conveys to others that you do not particularly care about yourself or about them. Of course, be clean and use fragrances sparingly. An overpowering perfume or lotion can repel, rather than attract, other people.

Others often see you more clearly than you see yourself. Good clothes, careful grooming, and consonant ✍ physical appearance provide outward evidence of an inner assurance. The effort to attend to your self-image is considerable. The payoff is commensurate ✍.

Record in the blank pages that follow or in your personal notebook any changes in your appearance that you may want to consider or attempt as a result of reading this chapter.

Summary

☞ Appearance and actions are key aspects of communication.

☞ Knowledge of body language can help you communicate more effectively.

☞ Certain facial expressions and body movements are associated with relatively precise cultural meanings.

☞ You can consciously modify your total appearance.

☞ Your appearance may affect your ability to accomplish your goals.

Eat to please thyself, but dress to please others.

– Benjamin Franklin

The outward form the inward man reveal, We guess the pulp before we cut the peel.
– Oliver Wendell Holmes

They (the English) think him the best dressed man, whose dress is so fit for his use that you cannot notice or remember to describe it.
– Ralph Waldo Emerson

Try to be like the turtle—at ease in your own shell.

– Bill Copeland

Why not be oneself? That is the whole secret of a successful appearance. If one is a grey-hound, why try to look like a Pekinese?
– Edith Sitwell

A winning smile is the best accessory any dress ever had.
– C. Terry Cline, Jr.

Your Ideas

_____

_____

_____

_____

_____

_____

_____

_____

_____

_____

_____

_____

_____

_____

_____

_____

_____

_____

To live content with small means; to seek elegance rather than luxury, and refinement rather than fashion.

– William Henry Channing

Your Ideas

_____

_____

_____

_____

_____

_____

_____

_____

_____

_____

_____

_____

_____

_____

_____

_____

_____

_____

_____

_____

_____

Beautiful faces are those that wear whole-souled honesty printed there.
– Ellen P. Allerton

Chapter 13

Organizing Meetings

Chance encounters sometimes profoundly affect humanity. One such encounter took place between two scientists on a commuter train in Germany in the early 1900s, and this encounter eventually led to the development of the Quantum Theory of Atomic Structure 📖. In turn came the search for new elements, the study of nuclear processes, the atomic bomb, and atomic energy plants. Not all meetings are as casual or as fruitful. However, most meetings could be considered culturally important.

As a progenitor 📖 of ideas, an instigator, a trailblazer, you will need to know how to organize meetings. Why? Shared ideas are more influential. Sharing hones 📖 ideas, sharpening, correcting, and modifying them. Those ideas that survive public scrutiny tend to inspire activity. In our complex society, lobbies and groups of people best effect change—even though the original spark usually comes from one person. Consider the history of environmental concern and the contributions of Rachel Carson 📖 and of Lois Gibbs 📖. Ms. Carson's book, *Silent Spring*, took a long time to have an effect on public attitudes about the environment. Lois Gibbs took the route of holding public meetings on Love Canal 📖 and had more immediate results with respect to environmental change. Of course, the influence of Rachel Carson's work probably made people more responsive to the efforts of Ms. Gibbs. Therefore, the difference in their methods was not the only factor affecting the results.

You, too, may have passionate beliefs that you would like to share in a public forum ᐧ. Have you considered the possibility of organizing a meeting with you as a speaker? You might be able to enlist others to present similar or opposing views. You might be able to arrange a public debate with the help of someone serving as moderator ᐧ. Ideas come from people and then become agents of change when they are publicly shared. If you really want to bring about change, consider meetings as a means of doing this. Even very small audiences can provide a useful forum for your ideas. Begin by discussing your ideas with your family and close friends. Seek their advice concerning sharing your ideas with other people.

Sometimes, the need to hold a meeting can arise quickly, so you might want to become aware now of the practical aspects of organization. Conventions and large-scale meetings require complex advance planning. But even the smallest sized meeting—two people—can be improved with some forethought. In your personal notebook, try briefly describing three or four topics that deeply interest you, along with a few questions or ideas you would like to explore. Then select one that could be a basis for a meeting. Try outlining a meeting plan using the following guidelines.

Purpose

Why should you hold the meeting? Think about the various things you wish to accomplish in the meeting. Is the purpose to discuss various points of view on a topic and then reach a decision? If the meeting is with one other person, is it to plan a collaboration ᐧ? To share techniques or strategies? If it is with a large group, is one of the purposes to introduce new members of an organization to veteran members? Is it to hear a speaker or a special presentation? Is it to plan an event and list each member's responsibilities? Is it to evaluate and then plan to improve something? Are you trying to solve a problem?

To hold a purposeful meeting, you should first be able to describe how each person will benefit by being present. Some meetings begin with a statement of purpose to keep participants focused on the task at hand.

When possible, circulate announcements and any needed background material to participants before the meeting. This helps people to come better prepared and saves valuable meeting time.

The best meetings encourage people to interact, develop ideas, and plan activities based upon a clear theme or purpose. Meetings generally provide a forum to present ideas with opportunities for discussion or other ways for participants to respond.

Suppose the purpose of the meeting is to share ideas with the members of your photography club about entering a new photo contest. To prepare, you make a list of important items to list on the agenda. You will want to note the application, categories, entry fees, judging criteria, and deadlines. You will also want to share the contest rules and allow time for discussion. You may want to divide the group into smaller groups to discuss entry categories and the feasibility of some or all members entering. To close, you may want to get a commitment from those who plan to enter and agree on a process for submitting entries for approval from the club sponsor before mailing. Thinking ahead of time about what needs to be accomplished within the time frame of the meeting will help you plan all aspects of the meeting.

If the purpose is simply to give announcements or routine dissemination ☞ of information, this is better done through a newsletter, mailbox flyer, or a phone message, rather than a meeting. People attending a strictly routine informational meeting may resent it, particularly if they feel they can use their time more profitably elsewhere.

Planning

You may benefit from the advice of someone who has had previous experience with the process of planning meetings. Pre-planning and thinking about the purpose will enhance the meeting results. Here are some additional planning questions to consider:

• How much notice must participants receive?

- What would be the best date? Will any holidays or other activities conflict with this date?
- Will facilities, needed materials, and speakers be available at this time?
- If a planning committee is needed, will the committee members have enough advance planning time?
- Is the meeting set up to allow reasonable amounts of time for each item on the agenda?
- Will someone be needed to take minutes of the meeting?

Participants

When planning a meeting, take a few minutes to consider who should attend. If the meeting is large, perhaps nametags would be beneficial. Also, if the meeting will be long, you may want to provide refreshments. A few more questions to think about include:

- Who should be there?
- How can they be notified?
- How can you find out who will attend, and later, who did attend?
- How will attendees benefit?

Publicity

Depending on the size of the meeting and the audience you want to attract, any of the following publicity approaches may be used: printed flyers, public address announcements, radio announcements, newspaper listings, printed or handmade posters, and/or press releases to news or print media. Consult someone with a background in journalism or marketing for the format to be used for press releases. You may be able to obtain sample press releases from other organizations.

Your publicity should include the title of the event, date, time, place, cost, and sponsor, if applicable. Including a map or directions to help people locate the meeting place might be useful as well. If you are using posters or signs, check with officials to make sure that your approach is acceptable.

Agenda

An agenda should be prepared for every meeting. It could be just for your own use or passed out to all participants. In preparing the agenda, ask yourself what would make you want to attend the meeting.

Make your agenda interesting by experimenting with size, shape, color, format, and content. Encourage participants to refer to it during the meeting, especially if the agenda is complex. At the very least, it will afford people a place to jot notes and/or doodle.

Facilities

Where will you hold your meeting? Are you sure the meeting place will be available at the time you want your meeting to occur? Select a place that is large enough and easily accessible for the participants. Seek out free facilities by checking public and semi-public institutions. You may need the help of a committee and the advice of a mentor for large meetings. Publicize travel arrangements, such as car-pooling and parking facilities. Keep in mind any equipment or materials needed, such as a TV/VCR or a chalkboard.

Problems

Be aware, ahead of time, of health and safety needs. Pre-plan substitute activities. Key people may be late to the meeting. Speakers may fail to arrive. Some meetings—or items on the agenda—may suddenly become impossible because of unexpected events.

Perfection is a rarity. When things go wrong, accept it as a challenge. Do the best that you can and remember to relax, smile, and enjoy your meeting.

Finale

The conclusion of every meeting should contain an opportunity to assess its value. Often this is done informally by briefly summarizing the meeting and asking for comments by the participants. Formal meetings featuring speakers frequently end with the distribution of evaluation sheets. If this is done, allow adequate time for their completion, collection, and review.

Write thank-you letters to guest speakers, sponsors, committee chairmen, and all who made contributions. If the news media were especially cooperative, make a special effort to express your thanks.

Arrange for a follow-up debriefing by a smaller group of participants. Ask the group members what actions should be the next steps after the meetings, and how such meetings might be improved in the future.

Keep records of the meetings that you attend or arrange. What worked? What irritated? How could you improve upon the design? What did you learn? How did you grow? What can you accomplish as a result of this meeting? When will you begin? Tomorrow?

Summary

☞ Meetings significantly affect human affairs.

☞ You can be an initiator of meetings.

☞ By following a guideline, the practical organization of meetings can be more effective and enjoyable.

Management by objectives works if you first think through your objectives. Ninety percent of the time you haven't.
– Peter F. Drucker

A chairman of a meeting is like the minor official at a bullfight whose main function is to open and close the gates to let the bull in and out. **– Dewey F. Barich**

Few people know how to hold a meeting. Even fewer know how to let it go.
– Robert Fuoss

Having served on various committees, I have drawn up a list of rules: Never arrive on time; this stamps you as a beginner. Don't say anything until the meeting is half over; this stamps you as being wise. Be as vague as possible; this avoids irritating the others. When in doubt, suggest that a subcommittee be appointed. Be the first to move for adjournment; this will make you popular; it's what everyone is waiting for. **– Harry Chapman**

The future is that time when you'll wish you'd done what you aren't doing now.
– Mary H. Waldrip

Use what talents you possess; the woods would be very silent if no birds sang there except those that sang best.
– Henry Van Dyke

Your Ideas

To know oneself, one should assert oneself. — **Albert Camus**

Your Ideas

_____

_____

_____

_____

_____

_____

_____

_____

_____

_____

_____

_____

_____

_____

_____

_____

_____

_____

_____

_____

_____

_____

_____

What we call results are beginnings.   **– Ralph Waldo Emerson**

Chapter 14
Public Speaking

Can you imagine someone with a speech impediment putting pebbles in his mouth and then talking loudly enough to compete with the roar of a stormy sea? (Doing this is not recommended). You might guess that this person must have had a great desire to be an orator ✍, and you would be right. Demosthenes 📖, the speaker, was the most famous of all Greek orators and a noted politician. He not only developed exceptional rhetorical ✍ skill, but also became known for his use of simple and appealing language. Although he lived from 383 to 322 B.C., many of his speeches are still available today and have influenced modern orators.

Essence of Good Public Speaking

The essence of good public speaking is having something worth saying and saying it with great care. Skill in doing this develops with practice. Some families set aside one mealtime a week for speech practice. Each member, on a rotating basis, selects a topic, prepares a five-minute speech, delivers it, and then directs the subsequent dinner conversation. If possible, try this, or try it with a group of friends.

Imagine that you have been asked to speak at a meeting. What an honor! What excitement! But how do you prepare? Enter the pertinent data—time, date, and place—into your personal calendar. Put reminder notes on the calendar at suitable intervals, such as two weeks before and one week before. Next, try to determine the needs and character of the audience. Why are you being asked to speak? If you are unclear, ask the person in charge. Discuss details carefully when the invitation is issued. How much time will you have to speak? Who will be in the audience? Is the purpose of the talk to inform, persuade, entertain, or a combination of these?

Once you have established the purpose, you should, of course, consider what exactly you plan to say. Try to anticipate what questions the listeners might have, and provide answers as you write your speech. Edit your material to fit the appropriate time. At a comfortable speaking rate, a 30-minute speech would require about 15 double-spaced typewritten pages—or two minutes per page.

Check Your Content for Clarity

Remember the audience probably knows less than you about this subject. There is a critical balance between saying too much and saying too little. Audience rapport tends to dwindle as a speech grows longer. It is better to leave your audience wanting more than wishing you had spoken less. In an informal speech, you can use audience reaction as a gauge of need for more or less detail.

A formal speech should be practiced for critique in front of people whose advice you value. If it is not feasible to practice your speech in front of a live audience, perhaps you can read your speech to someone over the telephone. Another excellent practicing technique involves using a large mirror and a video camera or tape recorder set near you. While being recorded, watch yourself in the mirror as you speak. How do you look? What kind of mannerisms do you have? After you finish, review the recording. How do you sound? What detracts from your ideas? Do your gestures match the points your words are saying? What needs to be changed? Which of your comments seemed most useful?

Consider Your Style of Speaking

An interesting speech will alternate between large views and detailed pictures, between generalities and specifics, between "soft focus and hard focus." These pictorial analogies are apt, for you are appealing to the visual acuity ᴇ⟋ of your listeners; their mental cameras are operating continuously, and you will want to present them with a picture through your words. Television depends on "technical events" to retain audience interest. These include changes in camera range and perspective. In a speech, reasonable transitions from the overview to the details have a similar effect.

Build Suspense During Your Talk

For example, at some point ask a question that you do not immediately answer. Throughout your speech, provide additional insights until the answer becomes almost obvious. Then let the audience discover it. Or you can incrementally ᴇ⟋ describe an unknown, then identify it as a climax. Or begin with impossibility, and gradually turn it into a possibility. Work out other variations if this approach appeals to you.

Use Language Creatively

Alternate simple language with the richness of an anecdote ᴇ⟋ or an allegory ᴇ⟋. Use the stimulating image found in a good metaphor ᴇ⟋. Develop clarity and impact with examples and analogies. You will be appealing to the creative thought processes of your listeners. View your speech as a gift package of your best ideas, wrapped in colorful language and presented with enthusiasm.

The bimonthly journal, *Vital Speeches*, is an excellent resource of recent speeches by people with established reputations in many fields, including politics, business, education, the arts, medicine, science, and law. These addresses can be examined for their technique as well as for their contemporary thinking on a wide range of topics. You will probably find certain styles that are more impressive, and these are the ones you want to emulate ⬿.

After Your Speech Is Written

Once your speech is written, now what? If you will be speaking for a long time, you may want to use a triple-spaced, large print copy completely edited with the exact wording that will be presented. You may wish to underline or highlight key phrases or perhaps write reminders to yourself to pause or look at the audience, etc. If your speech is less formal or shorter, bringing a list of words or ideas, sequential file cards containing major points, or a partial copy of the text containing any unusual enrichments (examples, metaphors, etc.) may be sufficient.

If a speech must be presented verbatim ⬿, do not completely read it to your audience. Try to memorize substantial parts of it. Look up as often as possible to establish eye contact with your audience. Pause frequently at key points during your speech. Fluctuate the loudness and emphasis of your voice. A monotone sound will bore your audience.

Often, the best speeches are extemporaneous ⬿, wherein the accidental interplay between audience and speaker creates a kind of magic. One idea leads to another so that even the speaker arrives at a mental destination previously unknown. Hopefully, this will happen to you at least once.

Whatever you can do to increase audience response and participation will be appreciated. The classic opportunities include applause and booing. Therefore, you may choose to build openings for audience participation into your speech. Ask the audience to do something at a subsequent point, perhaps to raise their hands, or to speak a key word or phrase.

Using "props" during your speech will make people savor ⬿ and remember each one of those minutes when you are speaking. Creatively think how you might use ordinary objects to highlight or exemplify parts of your speech. For example, choose a speech topic, and then see if you can figure out possible ways to use the following as props:

- a giant cardboard clock face with moveable hands
- a mirror
- a holder for large block letters plus extra letters
- a balloon
- large sheets of drawing paper, an easel, thick crayons, and a spotlight
- a wrapped package
- hats
- a hammer, a nail, and a board

After you are finished preparing your speech, you are still not done. Think about what you will wear on the big day. Choose comfortable clothes that are appropriate for the circumstances. Normally, avoid anything that looks bizarre. Low necklines, loud ties, or avant-garde ⌒ fashions are undesirable because they prevent the listeners from looking where they should be looking—at your face. Your clothes should permit simple, graceful movement. Tight or poorly fitted outfits create a poor image of you. Wear comfortable shoes. Remember, you will be standing for some time.

Speech Preflight Check

On the day of your speech, you have a few things to do before your big moment. Check all needed supplies and equipment before your departure. Leave enough time to arrive a bit early to double-check the arrangements. Make sure that you can use the microphone if it is provided. Have someone listen to you from various spots in the room to ensure that you are neither too loud nor too soft. Quickly test all of your audio-visual materials.

Before your speech, take a few deep breaths to calm down if you are nervous. When you are being introduced, remember that the audience will initially focus on your physical appearance. They will assess both your clothing and body language. Perhaps you are tempted to bolt out of a chair, grab the lectern, and rush into a torrent of words. Or maybe you slump as you walk toward the center of the stage, clear your throat, gulp, and with head bowed, read from a sheaf of papers that audibly rustle. Resist these tendencies. Instead, hold your head high, briefly acknowledge the introduction, and smile. Eye-sweep the audience with a face retaining some vestige of that smile, and proceed to speak.

Don't worry about sharp movements, paper shaking, and hands in the pocket, all of which indicate nervousness; audiences forgive and soon forget. Slumping, however, is a body language symbol for having no authority and the audience will tune you out. A bowed head bounces sound into the paper, not out into the room; the audience senses a lack of consideration and may label you as unqualified or egocentric. Standing tall with your head up denotes someone in command, with a "presence," someone to listen to and respect.

Remember why you are there speaking. Your ideas are being thoughtfully assessed by your audience. But if ideas alone were important, the print medium would suffice ⌒. However, speaking is a personal encounter. Therefore, you must, with all of your inner resources, project an image that demands attention and gains credence ⌒ for your ideas. Partly, you do this with an animated face. Look at the people. With a large audience, use eye sweeps—scanning slowly front to back, side to side. Occasionally stop and appear to speak directly to one person.

Focal Points While You Speak

As you begin your speech, check that the most distant group of people can hear you by using someone as a spotter with prearranged signals. Be similarly sensitive to problems with ventilation, noise, heat, and light. Uncomfortable people cannot listen accurately.

Your voice is very important. Irritating voices—high-pitched, nasal, whiny, raspy, whispery—are tuned out by the audience. Using breath control exercises often can ameliorate ⌒ these problems. (If this is a problem, library resources may be helpful.) Imagine that you are speaking to a very dear friend. Let your voice develop appropriate warmth and a "verbal smile." Changing tone and pitch makes subsequent words more important (this wakes up the audience). Avoid singsong accenting of words because it irritates most people. A rise in pitch at the end of a sentence makes you sound uncertain of what you are saying. Practice should permit you to attain reasonable pacing. Aim for a rate of about 150 words per minute.

If stage fright suddenly overwhelms you, pause and briefly contract your stomach muscles; keep them as tight as possible, then relax. Dr. Rozakis, in the *Complete Idiot's Guide to Public Speaking,* suggests: "Breathe from your diaphragm (your stomach) and through your nose. Don't breathe through your mouth." Look at one person in the audience, picking the friendliest possible face, and then keep going. The long-term best cure is practice. Eventually you will forget about yourself and become immersed *در* in your speech. Stage fright disappears.

At the end of your speech, close with a summation. If audience response has been invited, prepare to think fast. Answer questions as you are able, but also admit ignorance as honesty dictates. Try to diplomatically handle any persons who heckle or attempt to monopolize *در*. As you close your remarks, remember to thank the audience, your sponsors, and all the on-stage personnel. Where appropriate, send a written thank you note afterward to the person who invited you.

After Your Speech

A few days later, reflect on your speaking experience. How successful were you? How much did the audience respond? How could you improve? Maybe you will discover that you are a born speaker!

Try practicing these ideas by planning a speech on changes needed in your school or community. Summarize the results in the blank pages at the end of this chapter or in your personal notebook.

Summary

☞   A good speech contains worth-while ideas and is presented in a way that enhances the acceptance of those ideas.

☞   A good public speaker not only has a meaningful message, but also delivers it well.

☞   People can learn to be good public speakers, and public speaking improves with practice.

☞   A skillfully prepared content, a wisely projected personality, and a sensitive response to an audience will ensure success.

There is nothing in the world like a persuasive speech to fuddle the mental apparatus.
– Mark Twain

The finest eloquence is that which gets things done.

– David Lloyd George

We live in an age of words, of talk, of constant oral expression. Language is getting progressively looser. Oral expression is sometimes graphic, but is often flabby. It is almost always repetitive. Nobody can speak quite as well as he can write, certainly as well as he ought to be able to write if he doesn't tie himself into knots of affectation.
– Erwin D. Canham

I have just got a new theory of eternity.
– Albert Einstein (on listening to a long after-dinner speech)

Churchill wrote his own speeches. When a leader does that, he becomes emotionally invested with his utterances .... If Churchill had had a speech writer in 1940, Britain would be speaking German today.
– James C. Humes

Your Ideas

Eloquence is logic on fire.　　　　　　**– Lyman Beecher**

Your Ideas

_____

_____

_____

_____

_____

_____

_____

_____

_____

_____

_____

_____

_____

_____

_____

_____

_____

_____

_____

_____

A speech is like an airplane engine. It may sound like hell but you've got to go on.   **– William Thomas Piper**

Chapter 15
Five-Part Time

Like music, human activities also have a time aspect that can be managed well or poorly. Time is influential. The abrasive rub of time against human nature can be used to develop or destroy, just as sandpaper can smooth or scratch a piece of wood. What role does time play in your life? Do you artfully use it? Does it entangle you with unnecessary problems and aggravations? What questions about the use of time interest you?

Part 1
Construct Your Pattern then Consider Your Priorities

Invent, design, and implement a pattern to your life—a sense of what you will do and what you won't do. How much time will you allot for daily work, self-growth, human interaction, health maintenance, or charitable actions?

Consider some of the possible activities suggested to you in this book—maintain a calendar, keep a personal notebook, observe people, join an organization, practice speaking, read certain books, etc. Have you tried any? Think of all your daily activities, routine and otherwise. What did you do yesterday that makes today a better day? What will you do today? What should you do tomorrow? Consult your priorities—that personal shopping list for minutes, hours, days. *Critically* examine your desires, beliefs, and values. What choices have you been making? Do you want to change those choices? Set aside some quiet time and list those goals that are important to you now and into the future. Compare this list with your activities and goals that you may have recorded following Chapter 8 on Frustration. Are they consonant ᗡ? If not, what changes can you make? Try not to be blinded by custom or overly impressed by novelty and trends. Do some hard thinking. It is *your* life. Keep your lists of priorities and goals. Place them where you can view them frequently.

The previous questions are not easy to answer. But without these answers, your life may be a haphazard journey. No one else can better contribute to making your everyday life not just okay, but spectacular. There are only so many spring-times, friendships, and bursts of insight in anyone's lifetime. Anything can kindle your imagination and enjoyment. Be touched by the possibilities of a full life. Then determine the best way for you to develop a sensibly balanced use of time.

Part 2
Determination
and Persistance
Are Necessary

Occasionally you may be so inundated ᗡ with ideas that you can't find enough places to put them. Write them down so you can sift through this mental richness to find the good ideas—the ones that can be made to work. It is often said that ideas are cheap, but transferring those ideas into practice is not, precisely because it requires effort, and all labor has a price. If you **enjoy** thinking things up, you get an E for that kind of effort. When you can **conceive** of ways to implement ideas, you advance to a C grade. When you **begin** to convert ideas to action, you earn a B grade. When you **actualize** ideas, making them useful to others, you deserve an A grade. The latter requires persistence, and thus it is more highly valued. True persistence is uncommon; it has aspects of a devouring passion.

Just like the spider that must try many times to anchor a web, the inventor works long hours to succeed. Both have functional ability and determination. You, too, have abilities to function in many areas, but how do you develop the required determination? By assuming that you will be successful. Visualize success! Consider it to be a fait accompli ⌒. Whenever difficulties arise, return to this positive image. Then schedule work-time, organize materials, and begin. Do not try to solve everything mentally in a vacuum apart from physical productivity. Commit your ideas to paper, canvas, or other reproducible entity. In writing, your ideas are sharpened; in painting, your visions materialize reshaped; in making something, your hidden problems and advantages modify original concepts. Even the tiniest success feeds determination; the process is autocatalytic ⌒. Problems that develop become your incentive to find solutions.

You may be working at the edge of technical possibility because you may need something that doesn't yet exist or exists unknown to you. Talk to people, research the literature, and send out letters of inquiry. This is no time to freeze; try to do something.

Work intently. A natural tendency is to wander off target into distractions. Pencil tapping, a finger itch, thirst, or some pleasant daydreaming interrupt constantly. Discipline yourself by practice to minimize these distractions. Arrange the physical nature of your surroundings with this in mind. For example, some people work better with background music, while others require total quiet.

Finally, cultivate a stubborn streak. Refuse to quit. You may need to stop for a while, take a vacation, or pile up new resources. Start afresh, but don't give up!

**Part 3
Creatively Manage
Time Pressures**

Consider the following schedule selected by a writer:

The final draft must be ready by Tuesday, checked for grammar and sense by Wednesday, and a final copy must be produced by Thursday.

Problems with this schedule may occur. Some preconceived ideas require considerable effort to develop, and the time allotted for writing becomes insufficient. Deadline pressures may result.

Three solutions to this problem could be employed:

1. Time could be "stretched" by working more and by deleting nonessential activities.

2. Getting a fresh start or a new idea could help the writing flow more easily and the schedule may be met.

3. An alternate story with an easier topic could be written as a substitute. If meeting a deadline is important to you, you might consider using one of these techniques—time shuffling, a fresh start, or substitution—since they are often applicable when troubles arise.

How you handle deadline pressure, or any other pressure, is vitally important. You can best do this if you have a strong belief in your ability to cope, can respond sensibly to reality, are able to manage no matter what, and can responsibly accept pressures as a fact of life rather than as some diabolical ᐸᐳ persecution. Instead of thinking, "Why does this always happen to me?" begin realizing that life would be less interesting without challenges. Anne Morrow Lindbergh describes a useful inner harmony in her book *Gift from the Sea*: "But I want first of all—in fact as an end to these other desires—to be at peace with myself. I want a singleness of eye, a purity of intention, a central core to my life that will enable me to carry out these obligations and activities as well as I can."

That last phrase—"as well as I can"—is important. It can prevent the "paralysis of perfection." When you fear being foolish or making a mistake, and therefore fail to act, you are making the most foolish mistake of all—namely, failing to accomplish what is possible. This does not mean that you should be satisfied with whatever can be produced minimally. But it does mean that *your best* is good enough.

Initially, when starting a project, you have no absolute knowledge of the outcome of working on any problem. Snags may develop and may even leave you stymied ᐸᐳ. For these occasions, use creative thinking processes. Sometimes a mini-vacation helps. Close your eyes and take a mental journey; fantasize. Listen to music. When you really feel grim, picture your past successes. Imagine future success. Get up and walk around. Look out the window. Sort through mentally stored images—perhaps randomly. Look at whatever objects lie before you. Then, since problems don't usually solve themselves, go back to work. You may find reading *Peace of Mind* by Joshua L. Liebman useful.

Practical Strategies   Many practical strategies can help you achieve under pressure. Set up a schedule that permits certain checkpoints, what you expect to have completed at particular times. Make realistic estimates and then add, as a safety factor, a little extra time. You may need to assemble data, materials, and references as preparation for a particular task. Consider their availability *before* you make a deadline commitment. When your deadlines are set up by other people, try to understand clearly what steps will be involved. Realize that written statements, clear descriptions, and contracts about deadlines are desirable, not only to have a record of the agreement, but also to clarify expectations from others who may not share your way of thinking or have the same values. If their expectations differ from yours, try to think the problem through from their point of view even though this may be difficult.

If you have accepted a deadline, try to meet it honorably. Do the best you can. Since it is true that work tends to fill the hours allocated, you may find that limits actually improve your output. However, if you find you cannot meet a deadline, address the problem *immediately*. Ask for a postponement; get help; do something! Failure to act responsibly is the only real mistake. Learn from the experience. Pick up the pieces and go on. Separate this particular failure from a self-failure label. *You* are not a failure; you simply failed at doing *this*. People who try can fail. People who fail have a chance to learn. People succeed who learn from their mistakes.

Be aware of procrastination—the practice of not meeting obligations in a timely manner. It affects many people. For example, you may have friends who are habitually late for appointments. They overscheduled themselves, or became too involved in what they were doing, or simply delayed leaving in time for the appointment. In response, you try to compensate for their tardiness by setting an earlier-than-necessary time for their meeting you, in the hope that they will actually arrive on time. Although friends may make allowances for tardy habits, other people may be less accommodating.

If you are frequently late or fail to meet deadlines appropriately, you may want to evaluate ways to change these habits. They can affect your ability to achieve and to enjoy life. Consider why you are a procrastinator. Consider how you might change. On the next occasion that requires a timely response, make an all-out effort to meet this challenge. Don't abuse yourself if you fail. Just steadfastly persist, knowing that each success sets up a desirable mental connection. Dozens of these successes help you form a desirable habit. In all of these reactions to deadlines and on-time demands, you will be learning more about yourself and human nature.

Part 4
Appreciate
Your Patience

Patience is a virtue—and sometimes a pain in the neck. There is a human tendency to expect too much too soon because the mind leaps ahead. However, the spirit must endure all the barriers and indignities ᜂ that occur along the way. You may be a naturally impatient person. If so, choose work that yields quick satisfaction, and do not embark on a 50-year breeding program for shade trees! If you are at the other extreme, capitalize on your patience. Recognize the fact that it is a valuable trait, and select work that requires it. However, beware of excesses. The overly patient person may not realize when something is useless or no longer valuable. Conversely, the impatient person may hot-headedly quit before reaching goals. Either extreme can limit you from reaching your potential. Obviously, knowing your own proclivities ᜂ is helpful.

What is the difference between persistence and patience? Persistence implies a more active pursuit and continuous effort. Patience allows for time lapses between effort and results or permits nearly repetitive trials to reach a particular result.

Part 5
Make Time
for all the
Essentials

On the occasion of her hundredth birthday, a woman responded to a reporter's question, "What regrets do you have?" by quickly saying she wished that she had gone dancing and ridden the Ferris Wheel more often. You may think this to be a strange answer. But what if she had said, "I wish I had washed more dishes." Wouldn't that answer be stranger?

A balanced approach to life does include time for self-growth, work, human interaction, health maintenance, and charitable actions—and, of course, having fun. You can, and should, take pleasure in many activities, including those that the inexperienced person may deem frivolous ✍ . Remember that dancing is good exercise, a creative expression, and oftentimes an important cultural expression. Ferris Wheels, by design, offer the opportunity of an interesting view, as well as enjoyable sensations. But riding one also could give you the time to talk to a friend. Furthermore, sharing such recreational occasions with friends and family create memories that may give you strength during troubled times. All work and no play can diminish the quality of your achievements because of a narrowed vision of life or limit to self-growth and happiness.

Finally, one part of a reasonable time budget is often neglected—namely charitable actions. Giving enriches both the giver and the receiver. Unless you have always been an absolute hermit, you have benefited from the giving of a multitude of people. Those who have contributed to many publicly shared facilities such as schools, hospitals, libraries, art galleries, and radio and television stations have helped you—either directly or indirectly. Becoming personally involved in community enterprises by donating time (as well as money) is an essential quid pro quo ✍ in maintaining civilization.

You might want to examine your current use of time and record any desired changes in the following blank pages or in your personal notebook.

☞ Allocate time thoughtfully.

☞ Persistence gets the job done.

☞ Time pressures can be creatively managed.

☞ Habits of procrastination can be changed with effort.

☞ Patience and impatience affect your use of time.

☞ Set aside time for both pleasure and charitable actions.

Those who make the worst use of their time most complain of its shortness.
                                   – La Bruyere

Knowing trees, I understand the meaning of patience. Knowing grass, I can appreciate persistence.
                                   – Hal Borland

When I keep putting something off, it may not be procrastination, but a decision I've already made and not yet admitted to myself.
                        – Judith M. Knowlton

Procrastination is like a credit card: it's a lot of fun until you get the bill.
                          – Christopher Parker

In my youth I stressed freedom, and in my old age I stress order. I have made the great discovery that liberty is a product of order.
                                 – Will Durant

Your Ideas

There is a time to let things happen and a time to make things happen. **– Hugh Prather**

Your Ideas

_____

_____

_____

_____

_____

_____

_____

_____

_____

_____

_____

_____

_____

_____

_____

_____

_____

_____

_____

_____

_____

When one has much to put in them, a day has a hundred pockets.
– Fredrick Nietzsche

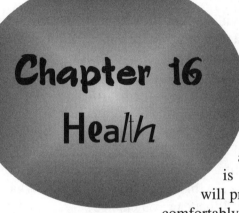

Chapter 16
Health

There is one absolute requirement for functioning as a human being—stay alive. A corollary &v concept is that your best functioning will probably occur if you can stay comfortably alive. But this can sometimes be a challenge.

You are a biological system made up of certain genetic codes and characteristics, some of which will probably remain unknown to you throughout your life. Important unknowns might be hidden factors such as genetic defects or inherited tendencies for certain diseases. Another unrecognized influence could be the impact of the physical environment on your health—the possible long-term influence of even minimally contaminated necessities such as air, water, food, as well as of the possibility of a sudden accident. A third factor is more directly controllable—namely your mental outlook, your attitudes, and your personality as they affect your lifestyle and ultimately your health. All of these factors—genetic inheritance, environment, attitudes, and behavior—can be managed to yield better health. But they can also be mismanaged.

Many people treat their personal health in a cavalier &v manner until threatened by some crisis. Often, more effort is directed toward maintenance of a car, or even a tennis racket, than toward self-preservation. On the other hand, too much concern with health, as exemplified ⤴ by the activities of a hypochondriac ⤴, can also be counterproductive. Consider the person who polishes a car daily, vigorously shining it. A shiny car is nice, but too much care can rub the paint away in what must certainly be an unintended result. Finding the right balance between carelessness and excess zeal is largely a matter of thoughtful experience. There are no simple guidelines to follow.

Self-Analysis

Knowing yourself will provide the best baseline for health care. Unfortunately, you were not born with a service care manual and therefore you will have to "discover" yourself. You are unique, but you also have commonalties with your peers. By observing the experiences of others, you can develop useful insights for improving your chances of living a long and healthy life. As a suggestion, find time to be quietly alone occasionally, and use this time for self-analysis. What are you doing that is sensible? What can you change?

Here are some questions to ask yourself:

- Do you eat breakfast every day?
- Do you eat three meals a day at regular intervals, with little snacking?
- Do you maintain desirable body weight?
- Are you getting regular exercise?
- Are you sleeping seven to eight hours each night?
- Are you avoiding using tobacco and alcohol?

Following these rules can not only dramatically increase your life span, but also make the quality of your life more enjoyable! The statistics strongly support the value of these sensible and simple rules. Many physicians and psychologists now note that behavioral factors such as these are the most important health factors facing people today and are ones that people can control themselves.

Behavior Health Problems   Some behavioral health problems may be even more important for you to consider because of your capabilities. You may, for example, feel that there are not enough hours in the day for you; you use time the way a desert soaks up a spring shower. It is exciting and wonderful to be able to do so many activities and to be so intensely involved. However, when people are preoccupied with many pressing tasks, they may be accident prone, with injuries as a result. Thus, under time-stress conditions, you may need to be particularly alert to managing potential behavioral health issues. You may, for example, decide to use public transportation, avoid driving a car in rush hour traffic, or arrange your travel time to be asynchronous ᐯ with potential accidents. For example, leave early to avoid heavy morning traffic.

You probably have a love of exploration, and may enjoy being the first to try, to do, to see. You may even like to live "on the edge." There is a strong likelihood that you are often successful in these ventures and greatly enjoy them. Initially, you may be blessed with beginner's luck, or you may triumph as a result of cautious planning and intelligent effort. The health-operative word here is "cautious." Exploration can be very hazardous. People who function at the edge of the unknown must be nimble of foot and wit to survive. Some do not survive. The lucky ones try again. Multiple successes can lead to a kind of fatigue carelessness. Precautions take effort, and eventually making the effort seems to be unessential when "nothing" happens. The chemist fails to use a safety shield for the hundredth time because nothing happened during the proceeding ninety-nine times. The explorer seeking new plant material in the Amazon jungle fails to check the snake bite supplies on his hundredth expedition. Guess what happens. Success can also lead to thinking that you are invincible. You think that you can instantly solve any problem because you know that you can solve many challenges easily. Caution does not imply that you need to retreat from the joys of exploration, only that you need to set out carefully.

Pay attention to clusters of accidents, such as breaking or losing things, falling, or hitting yourself. These may be signals of unresolved stress. Some introspection ᐯ would be appropriate.

You may be accident-prone because you are preoccupied with other matters. Then again, you may be unlucky, unobservant, or unwise.

Physical Health Problems Headaches may be a problem for you. Certain headaches can be very serious and require immediate medical attention, such as headaches increasing in intensity over a period of hours or days, headaches followed by a fever having no discernable cause, headaches accompanied by mental confusion, or headaches following any blow to the head. One excellent source of information on headaches is the book *Headaches, the Kinds and Cures* by Arthur S. Freese, D.D.S. Many headaches, annoying but not as threatening as those mentioned above, are physical responses to stress or emotional problems. These include migraines, tension headaches, sinus headaches, and depression headaches. Dr. Freese describes people likely to have migraine headaches as sensitive, compulsive, rigid, perfectionistic, having great pride in accomplishments, tending to suppress feelings of anger, hostility, or resentment, and being dependable, conscientious, and trustworthy. Since the age span typical for experiencing migraines is from 20 to 40 years, sufferers must either learn to either adapt or to diminish environmental stress occurring during those years. Headaches are debilitating—they prevent full functioning. If they are an affliction, you need to learn stress management techniques.

The concept of stress management has wider application than that of controlling headaches. Many years ago, a French psychotherapist, Emile Coue (1857-1926) 📖, advocated healing by optimistic autosuggestion. A typical self-affirming statement of this approach was, "I am getting better and better every day in every way." Psychotherapeutic treatment of a disease proceeds by mental suggestion. A.T.W. Simeon elegantly explores the psychological basis of many illnesses in *Man's Presumptuous Brain* . Illnesses can be physical manifestations of emotional problems, stress, and nervousness. Attempting to cure or ameliorate ↶ the physical symptoms without addressing the cause seldom produces lasting results. Therefore, learning how to manage your emotional state is at least as essential to your continued health as finding a good doctor.

Mental Health Problems

Everyone occasionally feels angry, frustrated, sad, depressed, worried, lonely, or uncertain. However, when these feelings persist and prevent your normal functioning, you may need to see your doctor. Other symptoms that may indicate the need for professional help include persistent moodiness, irritability, changes in appetite, sleeplessness, preoccupation with high-risk activities, intense concerns about physical appearance, or withdrawal from friends and family. Talk to a relative, teacher, counselor, or family doctor. The essential beginning to getting better is the willingness to admit to having a problem, then being determined to overcome it with help. Many mental health problems are common, well understood, and treatable. Your family doctor may be able to refer you to local counselor or therapist. There are many kinds of psychological therapies, such as psychoanalytic, behavior, cognitive, person-centered, group, and counseling. Choosing suitable help takes knowledgeable effort. An excellent library reference source is *The American College Physician's Complete Home Medical Guide*, edited by Dr. David R. Goldman (1999). This book has many informative sections on physical and mental illnesses. It also includes extensive on-line sites for many health agencies in the United States such the American Psychological Association at www.apa.org and the National Mental Health Association at www.nmha.org/index.cfm.

One mental illness that can be treated very successfully when properly recognized is manic-depression, also called bi-polar disorder. Among the famous people who likely had this disease are George Fredrick Handel 📖, Antonio Rossini 📖, Robert Schuman 📖, Honore de Balzac 📖, Vincent van Gogh 📖, Ernest Hemingway 📖, Theodore Roosevelt 📖, Winston Churchill 📖, Joshua Logan 📖, and Patty Duke 📖. Symptoms of this affliction commonly begin in the late teens to early twenties. Diagnosis often is based on recording alternating extremes of moods and behavior that go from very high and elated ("bouncing-off-the-wall") to very low and depressed (dark, somber, blue/black)—over a long period of time. This appears to be an inherited disorder, not controllable without medical help. An excellent book on the subject is *A*

Brilliant Madness, Living With Manic-Depression Illness, by Patty
Duke and Gloria Hochman. Ms. Duke relates her personal experiences with great courage and honesty. Alternating chapters provide
extensive information on probable causes, symptoms, and treatment of this disease.

The most advocated methods to prevent illness are dietary precautions, exercise, and elimination of the smoking habit. Obesity
has become a national health problem and is related to lack of exercise. Our modern conveniences entice us to be passively enter-
tained. It can be easy to sit in front of the TV or computer for long
periods of time, but try to take activity breaks such as walking the
dog or running around the block. It is important to eat thoughtfully, rather than by habit or simple convenience. Balanced diets that
are low in saturated fats and cholesterol are recommended.

Because the mind and body interact, psychological restoratives Ᏸ can effect a
wholesome personality, resistant to
somatic Ᏸ damage. Even though
you may not see yourself as being
flawed, you are likely to see potential
benefit in some suggestions for self-
improvement. Are they complicated suggestions? No. They are
disarmingly simple.

Self-Improvement Suggestions

- Smile.
- Make a conscious effort to really enjoy something
  each day.
- Slow down.
- Recognize that hostilities are a corrosive agent.
- Maintain interests in a wide variety of cultural
  activities.
- Actively seek to be with people.
- Listen.
- Avoid interrupting.
- Turn your attention to worthwhile tasks.

Your "container"—your body—has a tremendous range of physical, chemical, and physiological *structures. And like other living organisms, change in these structures is part of being alive. As you mature, major changes take place. Some of these changes are obvious and external; others are subtle and internal. The world around you likewise is continually changing. Your mental and emotional responses to changes influence your activities and total being for the rest of your life.

Be kind to yourself when calamity strikes or when any major change affects your life. Deaths, illness, job loss or change, moving, unusual success, loss of a friend—all of these can be stressful events. You should have strong feelings and be capable of expressing them, accepting the help of friends whenever possible. Consider the probable psychosomatic origin of any sudden health problems that develop during times of change and stress, and share your suspicions with your doctor.

Value life and take care of yourself. Care about others, for that is one root source of a stable psyche *. Refuse to yield to social pressures that can endanger you—no matter how persuasively expressed. This is particularly important because of the social use of drugs. Drugs (including alcohol) can be very risky and are directly and indirectly capable of causing irreversible damage to you, physically and mentally. Drugs are not necessary for expanding your mind. Any mind-altering should be accomplished by your conscious effort—not chemically induced. Recognize that health is related to the *quality* of your life—joyous, creative, and socially responsible.

Sexual experimentation can be extremely risky and have life-long health effects. Fortunately, you have the ability and enough common sense to choose how to behave responsibly. Of course sexuality is important to life, but it is not the totality of your being, nor that of anyone else. Any problems or questions concerning sex should be discussed with responsible family members, a physician, or similarly trustworthy people.

Many sexual variations exist, just as humanity has variability in hair color, height, and facial features. Labels such as heterosexual, homosexual, and bisexual do not describe anyone completely and should not be a source of discrimination.

Your birthright includes your right to control your health so that you can live more joyously. Here are a few other tips to help you. Try walking for exercise. Better yet, take walks with a friend. Take an umbrella if it is raining, and sing if you feel like it. Look at the puddles and the reflections. Feel the drops on your hands. It is good to be alive—simply—with no demanding expectations and no absolute disappointments. Hold onto an inner core of peace, a vision of a walk in the rain; look from a window onto a garden; see yourself opening a door to today, to tomorrow. Whatever may be your life span, your biological inheritance, or daily circumstances, if you value *being*, you will be comfortably alive.

Describe your health—mental and physical—in the pages following this chapter. Repeat this process at regular intervals, perhaps annually, and think about any changes.

Summary

☞ You can manage inheritance, environment, and behavior to obtain better health.

☞ Awareness of your self is essential to any realistic health program.

☞ Adhere to a few common sense health rules to achieve longevity.

☞ Carelessness and overconfidence can lead to accidents.

☞ Psychological wholesomeness may be your most important resource in achieving good health.

☞ Whatever may be your particular circumstances of well-being, enjoy each day as it exists.

Words of Wisdom

Suicide is a permanent solution to a temporary problem. **– Phil Donahue**

Man should not try to avoid stress any more than he would shun food, love or exercise.
– Dr. Hans Selye

The more serious the illness, the more important it is for you to fight back, mobilizing all your resources—spiritual, emotional, intellectual, physical. **– Norman Cousins**

(Today's students) can put dope in their veins or hope in their brains …. If they can conceive it and believe it, they can achieve it. They must know it is not their aptitude but their attitude that will determine their altitude.
– Jesse Jackson

Two out of every three deaths are premature; they are related to loafer's heart, smoker's lung and drinker's liver.
– Dr. Thomas J. Bassler

Brush them and floss them and take them to the dentist, and they will stay with you. Ignore them and they'll go away.
– American Dental Association

Coroners (they always have the final word) know why cocaine's nickname is killer.
– Dr. Joseph Pursch

Your Ideas

_____

_____

_____

_____

_____

_____

_____

_____

_____

_____

_____

_____

_____

_____

_____

_____

_____

_____

_____

_____

_____

_____

_____

_____

There are no such things as incurables; there are only things for which man has not found a cure. **– Bernard M. Baruch**

Your Ideas

For me, the creative process, first of all, requires a good nine hours of sleep at night .... **– William N. Lipscomb, Jr.**

> *We live in a time of such rapid change and growth of knowledge that only he who is in a fundamental sense a scholar—that is, a person who continues to learn and inquire—can hope to keep pace, let alone play the role of guide.* **– Nathan M. Pusey**

Chapter 17

Mentors

"It isn't what you know, it's who you know." This bit of folk wisdom is often true. If you collect contacts—people who can be helpful to you under special circumstances—the way other people collect knowledge of celebrities, you are being very wise. A modern term for this process is *networking.*

One special relationship that you should seek to establish is with a mentor. The origin of the word "mentor" stems from Greek mythology. Mentor was the friend of Odysseus 📖 who entrusted him with the education of his son Telemachus 📖. In modern parlance ᵔ, a mentor is someone who is a trusted counselor, guide, tutor, or coach.

Many mentor relationships develop naturally. Earliest mentors are admired family members who provide acceptable guidance while you are growing up. Other early mentors may be teachers, family friends, neighbors, and employers. These early relationships, even if they are short-lived, are often very influential. However, the most valuable mentorships develop as a result of careful thought and search. Think about what you wish to do. Think about your special interests. Who is likely to be knowledgeable in these areas and willing to share their expertise with you?

Locating a Mentor

Locating a suitable mentor will be a challenge, but there are some useful techniques. Perhaps you can ask your parents or a friend of the family who they might be able to introduce you to. Perhaps you can locate someone with established professional status through descriptions of their activities in newspapers. Often such persons win awards, organize conferences, become officers in organizations, publish, exhibit, and generally obtain public recognition for their achievements. It may be possible for you to attend public events where they are present. Contrive ⌒ to meet them, and try to make that meeting memorable. Write a follow-up letter expressing your interest in their work or ideas. Write a letter of congratulations for honors received, and include a brief account of your own aspirations. Ask for advice, and tell them you are looking for a mentor. You may be surprised to learn how accessible such people are and how willing they are to become mentors.

Many people will be flattered by your request and may wish to help you. Even so, some of them will be reluctant to accept the responsibility and time commitment that goes along with being a mentor. Do not apply pressure. You are seeking wise counsel and asking that it be freely given to you. Be realistic in your demands. As an unknown—the apprentice, the person at the bottom—you cannot expect people who are very busy to expend much time on your behalf. Make your questions brief, be very observant, and make your interest and appreciation apparent. Nourish any developing relationship by being thoughtful.

You may also find mentors through joining organizations that relate to your career interests and by becoming an *active* member. Accept committee work. Volunteer for tasks that will be shared with more experienced members. Do you admire someone? Ask them for counsel on appropriate occasions. When you find their counsel useful, tell them and thank them. When that experienced person voluntarily contacts you to give you suggestions, you will have found a mentor. To maintain this relationship, you will need social skill. What can you offer in exchange for the expertise shared and the connections supplied?

A mentor can locate unusual sources of information, provide guidance in technique, introduce you to other helpful people, and smooth the way for you to accomplish more with less effort. To achieve a good mentor relationship, you need to be willing to reveal both your desires and your abilities. Even in a good working association, you may occasionally need to tactfully reject advice. If you find yourself frequently rejecting advice, you need to carefully evaluate the relationship.

Mentors Can Help in Your Career Path

Being mentored may also help you in your career path. Suppose you have made a career choice but have no real idea of what that kind of work entails. Try to obtain employment in this area. It might just be a part-time job or an unpaid internship. For example, if you want to become a veterinarian, you might be able to obtain work providing routine care for animals. Almost all professional fields are associated with supportive service jobs. Find one of these and you can observe the professional work at closer range. These experiences provide you with a good chance to evaluate a potential career and possibly to find a mentor.

College students, including those high school students who take an occasional college course, have exceptionally good opportunities to locate a mentor. Professors usually are at the leading edge of knowledge within their field, enjoy sharing their knowledge, and are very influential. Any extra time spent in their company provides you a chance to learn and observe (like a tuition-free class). Some sagacious ⬥ students offer their assistance, paid or unpaid, in research endeavors just to obtain mentor benefits. Some of these relationships result in life-long personal and professional relationships.

Eventually, you probably will become employed and may need to know that many companies expect their professional personnel to make use of mentors. Sometimes neophytes ᧭ are assigned to someone who becomes their guide and guardian. The most astute ᧭ persons choose their mentor with a long view toward advancement. By alignment with someone " on the way up," you can achieve a coattail ᧭ effect and rise too.

Friends as Mentors

Mentoring can arise casually from friends sharing experiences. One friend is an experienced traveler and helps you plan vacations to exciting places. Another friend shares her expertise on theatrical events. Someone else becomes a guide on personal fitness. But you may at some point feel the need for new horizons to explore—a change in the focus of your leisure life.

You may want to develop a planned approach to expanding the range of people who can influence your life—using some of the same techniques suggested for obtaining career mentors. Seek people who seem to have special "joie de vivre," or joy of life. You may be able to establish an assembly of people from many backgrounds—including art, politics, science, young and old, rich and poor, like-minded and contentious ᧭—all able to socialize well. Such a group might meet infrequently with its structure and existence mutually established. Your normal circle of friends is derived from propinquity ᧭ , but the assembly you would be creating—a salon in the classic sense—is deliberately sought.

Contesse Marie Jeanne DuBarry (1743-1793) 📖 established a famous court circle or salon of artists and literary people. Alexander Woolcott (1897-1943) 📖 was the leading member of the Algonquin Round Table, which met in the 1930's in the Algonquin Hotel in New York City. Members of his group included Harpo Marx (comic/actor) 📖, Robert Benchley (actor, drama critic, and writer) 📖, Dorothy Parker (writer) 📖, George S. Kaufman (playwright) 📖, and others. Undoubtedly, many groups of a similar nature exist today. Perhaps the pleasant exchange (informal mentoring) about human experiences is a concept that you could explore.

Finally, whenever you can, become a mentor yourself. In the simplest sense, share what you know as freely as possible. "As ye give, so shall ye receive."

Summary

☞   Mentors can help you accomplish more with less effort.

☞   There are opportunities throughout life for the development of mentor relationships.

☞   Selecting mentors requires creative effort and social skill.

☞   Being a mentor is a worthwhile experience.

A good teacher has been defined as one who makes himself progressively unnecessary.
– Thomas J. Carruthers

No matter what accomplishments you achieve, somebody helps you.
– Althea Gibson

If you would thoroughly know anything, teach it to others.
– Tryon Edwards

If you have knowledge, let others light their candles at it.
– Margaret Fuller

To teach is to learn twice.
– Joseph Joubert

A great teacher never strives to explain his vision—he simply invites you to stand beside him and see for yourself.
– Rev. R. Inman

Your Ideas

Only a life lived for others is a life worth while. **– Albert Einstein**

Your Ideas

He that won't be counseled can't be helped. **– Benjamin Franklin**

> *There is only one success—to be able to spend your life in your own way.*
> **– Christopher Morley**

Chapter 18
Success

The limousine stalled just before the lift bridge. As the chauffeur endeavored to find the trouble, the grey-haired passenger emerged and strolled toward the little shack of the bridge-tender.

"What a surprise! What are you doing here?"

The man looked up from his book and slowly replied: "Reading."

His tiny wooden table was cluttered with books, scraps of paper, and the remains of a paper bag lunch.

The visitor, looking closely at the bridge-tender, asked: "Do you remember me? Weren't we classmates at Yale?"

The bridge-tender nodded in agreement.

"Then why are you here?"

"It gives me the time to do what I enjoy most of all—read."

With this reply, he went back to reading his book—oblivious to the shock on the face of this visitor.

Who do you think made better use of his education or his life? Who is more successful? Why? Can you really tell from such a simple account? Does it matter?

Success is one of the magic words of modern society. There are commonly accepted standards of success, but there is also an aura ᘒ of private meaning. It is this private meaning that tends to become our lifetime guide. Take time to reflect on what "success" means to you. You might do so by completing each of the following statements, either below or in your personal notebook.

1. Among my immediate acquaintances, _____ is most successful because _____ _____.

2. Among the famous contemporaries known to me, _____ is most successful because _____.

3. Among all historically famous people known to me, _____ was the most successful because _____ _____.

4. I'll feel successful today if _____ _____.

5. I'll feel successful this week if _____ _____.

6. I'll feel successful this year if _____ _____.

7. At the end of my life, I'll feel successful if _____ _____.

8. To be successful, I need to _____ _____.

Did you find answering the questions challenging? Was it difficult to select successful people? How did you react to thinking about your own success? What were your feelings as you read the vignette ᘒ?

The nature of success can be ambiguous ᘒ. Think of the bridge-tender and the man in the limousine. One person's success is another person's failure. By examining the nature of success as currently perceived, you can develop your own concept of success—what it is, what it is worth, and how to achieve it. You can't examine success quite as easily as you can study a leaf or a stone, but you can apply some of the same principles of scholarship. In fact, if you answered the questionnaire, you have begun the process.

The second phase of studying success could reasonably involve surveying the literature.

The following descriptions of some "success" books may be useful for you. If you are interested, read them.

1. *Skills for Success: A Guide to the Top for Men and Women*, Adele M. Scheele, Ph.D. (1996). Dr. Scheele's book is inspirational; it describes career competencies that would be useful in *many* areas, and it makes success an ethical imperative. In-depth interviews with Ely Calloway 📖, Dom DeLuise 📖, John Brooks Fuqua 📖, and Shirley Hufstedler 📖 provide illustrations of Dr. Scheele's premises.

2. *Ambition: The Secret Passion*, Joseph Epstein (1980). Mr. Epstein provides an erudite ∿ voyage through America's history, highlighting it with short biographies of illustrious Americans. The epilogue ∿ is especially interesting.

3. *Live for Success*, John T. Molloy (1981). The author offers practical advice on his specialty—appearance—as well as on functioning at job interviews, public meetings, and in various office situations.

4. *The Sky's the Limit*, Dr. Wayne Dyer (1980). The author explores the psychological basis for success in great detail. Many of Dr. Dyer's ideas mesh with those in Dr. Scheele's book even though the perspective is different, and success in a traditional sense is not the main topic.

5. *What's Holding You Back?: 8 Critical Choices for Women's Success*, Linda Austin (2000). Dr. Austin provides professionally derived insights into the achieve-

ment process for women. Although this practical information is especially useful for women, it is also valuable for men who share the working world.

6. *Success is a Choice: Ten Steps to Overachieving in
Business and Life*, Rick Pitino with Bill Reynolds
(1997). Using many examples from his experience as a
basketball coach, Mr. Pitino develops ten specific techniques for achieving success. This motivational
approach is easy to read.

7. *The Seven Habits of Highly Effective People: Restoring
the Character Ethic*, Stephen R. Covey (1989). This
work, a probable classic in the literature of success, contains elegant assessments of a principle-based approach
to achievement. A "must read" book.

8. *Life Strategies: Doing What Works, Doing What
Matters*, Philip McGraw (1999). This is an intensely
personal examination of how people can view and
assess themselves, others, and life in order to achieve
goals, happiness, and success. This realistic study of ten
significant common characteristics of people is accompanied by interesting examples of behavior.

The third phase in your scholarly study of success is to actively pursue a course of action. Why not try it? Write a book, a paper,
or a poem. Paint a picture. Write a sonata ♫. It might not be perfect product, but if you finished it, then you have succeeded! List
some successful people you would like to know more about, using
the blank pages that follow this chapter. Follow up with information
you discover concerning one of your choices.

Summary

☞ Start where you are, look around at what you have and what you can use, and launch a dream. No place is too small to begin.

☞ Consider the probable requirements for the type of success you desire. Can you realistically meet them?

☞ Work hard, not in isolation, but in the context of a richly varied and sometimes supportive human community.

☞ Take calculated risks. If failure occurs, learn from it and proceed.

☞ Develop patience with uncertainty, imperfection, and ambiguity ᴇ⌢.

☞ Consciously, and sometimes subconsciously, use your knowledge and experiences to cultivate yourself. Learn and grow.

☞ Prize your existence as a human being—pay dues by being responsible and concerned for your compatriots ᴇ⌢.

☞ In the long run, honesty always pays.

☞   Look ahead; for example, don't rush from one traffic signal to the next. Use timing and alternative routes.

☞   Be more anxious to *accomplish* than to be a "success," to garner awards or rewards.

☞   The classic advice "Find a need and fill it" usually works.

My mother drew a distinction between achievement and success. She said that achievement is the knowledge that you have studied and worked hard and done the best that is in you. Success is being praised by others, and that's nice, too, but not as important or satisfying. Always aim for achievement and forget about success.
                                    – Helen Hayes

Success is that old ABC—ability, breaks, and courage.   **– Charles Luckman**

No one can possibly achieve any real and lasting success or "get rich" in business by being a conformist.
                                    – J. Paul Getty

Pick battles big enough to matter, small enough to win.
                                    – Jonathan Kozol

The tragedy of life doesn't lie in not reaching your goal; the tragedy lies in having no goal to reach.
                                    – Benjamin E. Mays

If I have been of service, if I have glimpsed more of the nature and essence of ultimate good, if I am inspired to reach wider horizons of thought and action, if I am at peace with myself, it has been a successful day.
                                    – Alex Noble

Your Ideas

_____

_____

_____

_____

_____

_____

_____

_____

_____

_____

_____

_____

_____

_____

_____

_____

_____

_____

_____

_____

_____

_____

Strive not to be a success, but rather to be of value.

– Albert Einstein

Your Ideas

_____

_____

_____

_____

_____

_____

_____

_____

_____

_____

_____

_____

_____

_____

_____

_____

_____

_____

_____

_____

I haven't failed. I have successfully discovered 12,000 ideas that don't work.   **– Thomas Edison**

> *No pessimist ever discovered the secrets of the stars, or sailed to an uncharted land, or opened a new heaven to the human spirit.*
> **– Helen Keller**

Chapter 19
The landscape of Courage

The landscape of courage is uneven. Life inevitably will contain moments of fear, but your quick strokes of strength can help you meet these challenges with competence.

It is the management of everyday life that nourishes the roots of courage. Getting up, getting going, and getting to use—not abuse—each day takes courage. It takes inner strength to push outward, be with people, pursue tasks, make decisions, live with the results of those decisions, loosen ideas into the public domain, have those ideas judged, learn to perform, and be tested. It is easier sometimes to stand still, be a child, be cared for, withdraw, and do the minimum. It is truly awful to watch the parade pass by from a hole in the ground, to so limit extension and involvement that the viewing-eye level is on the pavement. Holes can only be "safe" if nothing falls in.

There is a blood, thunder, and glory version of courage. Its usual source of courage is fear—physical or social—so intense that adrenaline flows and action is possible. Revolutionaries, battle participants on war maneuvers or in boardrooms, race car drivers, and contestants of all kinds have a need for courage. This kind of valor can light up the sky with its intensity briefly, like firecrackers.

- You may be saying: "When the time comes, I'll be ready."
- You may be saying: "How will I know what to do?"
- You may be saying: "I'll never know until something happens."
- You may be saying: "Just try me."

But courage is not limited to those occasional feats of perilous Ꮔ lifesaving. Actions under the white, hot glare of instantaneous need, such as pushing the child away from an oncoming car, are important fodder Ꮔ for newspaper headlines precisely because of their rarity. Though some rescue actions may be deliberately courageous, others may actually be acts of cowardice. Some rescue responses may be almost reflexive, as a result of social conditioning. An interesting evaluation of certain situations is given in Ayn Rand's book, *The Virtue of Selfishness*.

There are no training institutes for courage, although one could argue that both the armed forces and sales training schools build toward it. There are no technical manuals that explicitly prepare you to be courageous. However, there are many inspirational books which treat courage as an important human trait. One example is *Peace of Mind* by Joshua L. Liebman; its chapter on fear provides an antithetical Ꮔ treatment of courage.

But knowing what courage is does not automatically make one courageous, just as reading about chocolate is not the same thing as tasting it. Is there any day when courage is not needed? Is today your day to taste courage? Will you meet the challenge?

Thomas Carlyle 📖 said, "Depend upon it, the brave man has somehow or other to give his life away." At face value, this implies that bravery is associated with risking death. But bravery cannot mean only replacing one life with another. From another viewpoint, Carlyle could be suggesting that bravery is associated with risking *life*. How? By living so as to give away something of value to others, by creating, by accomplishing. By living to this extent, you give your life away. Such living has a purpose that exceeds self-maintenance. It is valorous Ꮔ.

Every part of daily existence has some opportunity to be brave, take chances, extend yourself. If you want to launch a courageous life, look within yourself and examine your personal beliefs; then act in accordance. President John F. Kennedy's *Profiles in Courage* describes instances of political courage. The last few paragraphs of the *Young Readers' Memorial Edition* of this book are worth remembering:

> *For, in a democracy, every citizen, regardless of interest in politics, 'holds office'; every one of us is in a position of responsibility; and, in the final analysis, the kind of government we get depends upon how we will fulfill those responsibilities. We, the people, are the boss, and we will get the kind of political leadership, be it good or bad, that we demand and deserve.*
>
> *These problems do not even concern politics alone—for the same basic choice of courage or compliance continually faces us all, whether we fear the anger of constituents, friends, board of directors or our union, whenever we stand against the flow of opinion on strongly contested issues .... The courage of life is often a less dramatic spectacle than the courage of a final moment; but it is no less a magnificent mixture of triumph and tragedy. A man does what he must—in spite of personal consequences, in spite of obstacles and dangers and pressures—and that is the basis of all human morality.*
>
> *To be courageous ... requires no exceptional qualifications, no magic formula, no special combination of time, place and circumstances .... In whatever arena of life one may meet the challenge of courage, whatever may be the sacrifices he faces if he follows his conscience—the loss of his friends, his fortune, his contentment, even the esteem of his fellow men—each man must decide for himself the course he will follow. The stories of past courage can define that ingredient—they can teach, they can offer hope, they can provide inspiration. But they cannot supply courage itself. For this each man must look into his own soul.*

There are probably some things that you are sensibly and rightly afraid of and other things that you are foolishly and unreasonably afraid of. There are life-preserving fears, such as fire, falling, or drowning. There are life-stultifying *&* fears, such as meeting people, taking tests, or public speaking. Regardless, knowing how to handle your fears is useful. Is there a method or strategy that works?

The following example is a fantasy, based partly on modern research into the nature of the mental activities of people. *Psychofeedback*, by Paul G. Thomas, is an excellent book to read in this area of mental operations.

> *Octavia, the fourth child of the family, had been left behind. She awoke, looked at the blackened door, and fear tumbled through her. Eventually she pried away a piece of carbonized wood and, using a scrap of paper found on the floor, wrote the following:*
> *Today, I live, explore.*
> *Tomorrow, I do what I can.*
> *Each day is very good.*
> *Then she began her meditation exercises. With her mind and body in a relaxed but sharply receptive mode, she deliberately thought of previous good times. Holding her three-line note, she read it aloud, thought about it, and read it again. She thought about the qualities she would need to survive what was on the other side of that door—determination, flexibility, caution, confidence, and courage, especially courage.*
> *At nineteen, this "child-no-longer," knew that courage turned on the biocomputer—but that the biocomputer had to be carefully programmed so as not to fail the operator and convert her to a statistic.*
> *Finally, she signed off. "I'm alive, vibrantly alive. I am capable and I can manage. One, nine, eight, four, awake."*

You have to push open your own door to find the landscape. The latchkey is hard to find and the opening may be small. But once you step away, you won't want to stop. And almost nothing will stop you.

Write a brief account of the most courageous act that you have ever witnessed, using the following blank pages or your personal notebook. Add other occasions as you discover them, and review them periodically.

☞ Courage is essential to thoughtful daily living.

☞ Collective acts of courage have made civilization possible— even for the cowardly.

☞ The *habit* of courage can be internally programmed.

**Words
of
Wisdom**

All serious daring starts from within.
– Eudora Welty

The time when you need to do something is when no one else is willing to do it, when people are saying it can't be done.
– Mary Frances Berry

Everyone has talent. What is rare is the courage to follow the talent to the dark place where it leads.
– Erica Jong

Courage is very important. Like a muscle, it is strengthened by use.
– Ruth Gordon

Courage is doing what you're afraid to do. There can be no courage unless you're scared.
– Edward V. Rickenbacker

Give me the serenity to accept what cannot be changed. Give me the courage to change what can be changed. And the wisdom to know one from the other.
– Reinhold Neibuhr

I have had dreams, and I have had nightmares. I overcame the nightmares because of my dreams.
– Jonas Salk, M.D.

Your Ideas

_____

_____

_____

_____

_____

_____

_____

_____

_____

_____

_____

_____

_____

_____

_____

_____

_____

_____

_____

_____

_____

_____

The courage to imagine the otherwise is our greatest resource, adding color and suspense to all our life. **– Daniel J. Boorstein**

Your Ideas

Why not go out on a limb? Isn't that where the fruit is?

– Frank Sailly

Chapter 20

Lotion, Sandpaper, and a Tin Cup

What do lotion, sandpaper, and a tin cup have in common? As you will see, all three are important interpersonal metaphors.

As animal brain size increases, so does the complexity of behaviors and interactions with others. Thus, "bird-brainedness" to describe someone's thoughtless behavior is a verbal realism as well as a peculiar epithet ᔕᕐ. The incredible richness of brain functioning in humans also supports an equally rich and complex structure of behavior. It is important to know the vocabulary of human behavior so that you can be more comfortable in complex social interactions, feel at ease socially, and help others feel the same way. Probably the best way to achieve this degree of behavioral savoir-faire is to develop your ability to think consistently of the needs and desires of others.

Imagine you face a friend who, you realize, believes you have forgotten to return her book. Her face has a tense look and you see the anger even before she speaks. To defuse the situation, you cover your face with your hands, then peek around the edges of your fingers. She laughs at your gesture and relaxes, and you then cautiously laugh; a few succeeding words solve the problem. In fact, you tell her, you returned her book when she wasn't home. Your ability to sense the thoughts, attitudes, or feelings of another person is called empathy; it is the human trait most responsible for soothing the stresses of human interaction. Reading body language, assessing a tone of voice, noting mannerisms helps everyone respond with better awareness to other people, and is a lotion that allows our interactions to flow smoothly!

Good Manners — the Lotion of Human Society

Successful diplomats and politicians usually have extraordinary empathetic skills. The words polite and politician share common Greek and Latin word origins. Richard Gephardt's book, *An Even Better Place: America in the 21ˢᵗ Century*, presents cogent ⌖ arguments concerning how to make political structures more effective. He states: "Thus, mutual respect and civility among members of Congress aren't merely desirable; they are the only *practical* basis upon which our government can be run."

Unfortunately, just wanting to do the right thing and really caring about others may not be enough. Often we must know the elaborate rules for certain social occasions that do exist within our society. Although most rules of social etiquette reflect common sense attitudes toward the best ways for people to interact, some rules may appear to be silly or irritating. Some of the silly ones are probably vestigial ⌖ remnants of behaviors needed in the past. Some of the present male-female rules are of this type. Other rules are maintained to identify class members—upper, middle, and lower. Communities also tend to develop certain customs that are useful in identifying "belongers."

On occasion, you may break the social rules, whether knowingly, carelessly, or possibly as a result of ignorance. Others around you usually will have negative reactions when you do. As a penalty, they may subsequently exclude, avoid, or try to limit you. At first glance, social rules may seem stifling. Surprisingly, though, living by the rules generally tends to permit more personal freedom than would occur by ignoring rules.

Become an Observer

How do you learn the lotion rules? Become an observer. Emulate ⌢ people who have good social grace. Also analyze successful and unsuccessful situations, and use your insights to develop sensible and sensitive behavior. Good manners can defuse tense situations. Also, concern for the other person's point of view tends to produce a reciprocal effect. A smile, a handshake, and pleasantries about family or circumstances can make any social event better for both you and others.

The Written Word

In an age of easy verbal communication, the promptly written thank you note has a special cachet ⌢. Assemble a stationery folder and fill it with an assortment of notepaper, cards, and stamps. Correlate ⌢ the quality of your stationery with the circumstances of its use. Then write as often as possible—to express gratitude, congratulations, acceptance, a point of view, etc. Skill develops with practice. Libraries have entire books on how to write letters for most occasions. The important thing to remember is that letter writing is not only a valuable art, it is a necessary adjunct ⌢ to desirable social behavior. Appropriate social behavior is important to the work culture of many organizations.

Be Willing To Abide by Etiquette

You may be judged critically at some important point in your life on what may appear to be a nonsensical set of rules—namely, table manners. Consider what is meant by being *willing* to abide by etiquette. For example, there is no absolute functional necessity for placing forks tine-side-down on your plate when you have completed a course. It does, however, provide a silent signal to the waiter. It marks you as being a knowledgeable person and a conformist in an area where conformity has little or no philosophical overtones, but rather has a practical communication value. Thus, observance of table manners and other rules of etiquette provide a clue to character and intelligence and can also make events more positive than they otherwise might be.

A bit of "when in Rome, do as the Romans do" often applies to the social scene—there must be a reasonable matching of behavior to the circumstances. Otherwise, you may unintentionally be offensive. You do not use fingerbowls 🔖 at a picnic, but you should learn how to use them in preparation for a very formal dinner.

Rudeness — the Sandpaper of Human Society

If good manners are the balm and lotion of human society, rudeness is the sandpaper. Not that rudeness is without value. There may be occasions when deliberate rudeness is useful—but such occasions are very, very rare. For example, Anne's friend Tara constantly interrupts her— even when others are present. Anne would begin, "Next Thursday I think we should ..." and Tara would interrupt, "Why next Thursday?" Initially, Anne tried humor as well as both gentle and firm direct requests to Tara to stop her irritating habit—all ineffective. Finally, Anne succeeded, though it required a firmness that was somewhat rude. At a small committee meeting, Anne's words were cut off as usual. Then Anne spoke loudly and with slow emphasis, "Since Tara knows what I am going to say before I do, I think that she is capable of doing my work before I do. Therefore, I vote that Tara be assigned both writing notices and all telephone calling. All agreed? Good. Motion carried." Tara for once was speechless.

You do not, however, want to be rude unintentionally. Is there a possibility that you sometimes are unwittingly offensive to others? Even your best friend may be unwilling to tell you that you have unpleasant mannerisms. Interrupting a speaker, being inattentive, not returning letters or phone calls, toying with table implements, rocking on dining chairs, putting feet on furniture, snapping gum (or chewing it publicly), monopolizing conversations, not returning greetings, forgetting to say thank you or send a note, not meeting obligations, and failing to treat *each* person as you would wish to be treated—all of these habits are abrasive and deleterious 🔖 to your social success.

Attend to the Little Things

Attend to the little things, for it is often the small behaviors that describe and give color and flavor to human nature. Thomas Jefferson 📖, in designing Monticello 📖, made the staircases very narrow—too narrow to permit comfortable passage for any woman in the wide skirts of that time. The implication is that he did not act considerately with respect to the needs of the women in his household. In many other instances, especially when entertaining guests, he was a thoughtful person. Flaws are a part of human nature. You should try to eliminate your own sandpaper flaws as they become obvious, but do not expect perfection. Thomas Jefferson was an exceptional statesman, a creative architect, and a much-admired host. He was not perfect.

Sometimes friction arises because you expect others to act in a certain way—but they may have a different idea. The modern glib 𝒢 answer is that a communication problem exists, and this may be true. But other possibilities exist as well. Your expectations may be unrealistic; they may, in fact, be impositions. For example, you may expect your best friend to take care of your pet dog while you are on vacation. You have explained how to feed and exercise the dog and when you will be back. When you return, you find a jubilant 𝒢 pet but a resentful friend who cancelled other opportunities because of his duty to your dog. From this point onward, your friendship deteriorates 𝒢. Why? Your friend was very busy and didn't have the time for the job, but had not been candid 𝒢 enough to say no. For someone else who had more free time, your expectation would have been reasonable. You would need the sensitivity to discern the difference or to ask in such a way that the friend could say yes or no comfortably.

The Tin Cup — Gratitude in Human Society

With practice, you will have fewer occasions of interpersonal friction and more pleasant relationships where the lotion is present. Often, such smooth interactions will result in gratitude. However, two ideas concerning gratitude are particularly valuable. One, do not expect it—*ever*—or you may find yourself rattling your tin cup in vain like a beggar in a desert. Instead, do things simply because they are good and need to be done, not because you expect a reward. Two, express your gratitude to others whenever possible.

To put these ideas in perspective, consider your own experience. Have *you* thanked everyone who made a special effort on your behalf? If not, why not? Did you secretly carry your feeling of gratitude? That is very normal. Now think about occasions when you helped others but did not receive any recognition for your efforts. That, too, is very normal. But how did you feel? Were you encouraged to continue and to do more, or were you discouraged?

Would you like to add a bit of improvement to the world?

Put Yourself in the Other Person's Shoes
Imagine that you are the other person, and respond accordingly. Put yourself in the other person's shoes. A simple verbal thank you, such as, "I appreciate the time you gave me," a note of appreciation, a spontaneous return of a favor are welcome responses to favors received. Let your sensitivity extend to *everyone* who affects your life—not just those who are powerful, or important, or who might give you special treatment.

Begin today if this is not already your modus operandi ☞. People will be delightfully surprised and your own life will be richer. Finally, one additional valuable aspect of gratitude is its ability to nourish excellence of behavior. By telling someone that you appreciate what is being done, you provide encouragement for them to continue that behavior.

So what do lotion, sandpaper, and tin cup have in common? They can symbolize human reactions to other people—good manners, rudeness, and gratitude. Your style of interaction will affect others as well as yourself. Of all the multitude of possible behaviors, how often have you selected behaviors that were good etiquette? What about your future choices?

Write your personal reactions to the contents of this chapter in the following blank pages or in your personal notebook.

- ☞ Learn and use the rules of etiquette.

- ☞ Manners are not simply social veneer 〰; they are the foundation of social interaction.

- ☞ Careful observation of people can lead to improved social skills.

- ☞ Deliberate rudeness can be desirable on occasion.

- ☞ Confer gratitude frequently; expect it rarely, if at all.

Do good to thy friend to keep him, to thy enemy to gain him.

– Benjamin Franklin

Rudeness is the weak man's imitation of strength.

– Eric Hoffer

Civility costs nothing and buys everything.
– Lady Mary Wortley Montagu

Life is short, but there is always time for courtesy.

– Ralph Waldo Emerson

And so, my fellow Americans: Ask not what your country can do for you—ask what you can do for your country.

– John F. Kennedy

Behold, I do not give lectures or a little charity—when I give, I give myself.

– Walt Whitman

Your Ideas

_____

_____

_____

_____

_____

_____

_____

_____

_____

_____

_____

_____

_____

_____

_____

_____

_____

_____

_____

_____

Love your enemies, for they tell you your faults.
– Benjamin Franklin

Your Ideas

Each day comes bearing its gift; untie the ribbons.

– Anne Ruth Schabacker

Chapter 21
Ambition's Gamble

One possible outlet of ambition is employment. Employment can supply the necessities of life, some luxuries, a source of self-esteem, and an opportunity for creative expression. The parameters ↩ of each of these possible outcomes derive, in part, from your ambitions. At various times in your life you may seek work just to earn money, with little regard for the learning that can take place or the satisfaction value of a good job. Summer jobs and part-time work may be examples of this kind of employment. But a career search usually is undertaken with greater care because you are attempting to satisfy a larger range of needs. You have to understand yourself and your ambitions to make career choices. What do you know about seeking employment? How do you intend to satisfy your ambitions?

Seeking Employment

Getting a job can be like assembling a complicated object with the aid of an enclosed diagram. The diagram looks simple, the parts are simple, but at first, they simply don't go together. Reality butts in—primarily as a result of inadequate information. Eventually, persistence pays off and the assembly occurs. The same thing can happen in seeking employment.

The following accounts briefly detail the work experiences of six very talented young people. As you read them, think about your own circumstances.

- Fred found a summer job working as a gardener's assistant. He showed up for work on the first day with a radio and hung it on a nearby tree. It blasted out rock music, startled birds, and ruined neighborhood tranquility. Fortunately, he was perceptive enough to leave it home the next day—or he would have lost a job, which he came to enjoy deeply.

- Rafael couldn't get any summer work locally, but obtained a job as a waiter in a distant summer resort. His appearance, willingness to work hard, and good humor impressed several influential guests. He not only accumulated enough money through tips for his first college semester, but he also made personal contacts useful for future employment.

- Upon graduation from high school, Tamika found a job as a receptionist-typist in a small office near her home. She felt trapped and bored within two months.

- After carefully surveying his aptitudes and desires and obtaining appropriate college training, Roy went into the computer repair business for himself. He is now president of a company at the leading edge of a growing industry.

- Almost through high school, uncertain of career direction, Amelia feels a bit frightened. Part-time work in her chosen field of cosmetology has been unsatisfactory.

- Making use of talents in several areas, Christine has become an author and has achieved a high-ranking job in the banking industry.

The following comments are offered on each of the above examples.

- For your first job, people older than you are likely to do the hiring; therefore, sensitivity considering their attitudes and values probably will be essential to becoming employed. Fred's use of the radio, while acceptable and sensible from his point of view, was offensive and unreasonable to his employer. It indicated a frivolous ↝ attitude toward work. Even a good worker, if irritating, will eventually be fired. Appearance, mannerisms, and speech habits can affect employment. Employers judge employees both by outward appearance and what they can accomplish.

- Both Fred and Rafael made good use of their summer earnings; in each case they obtained college degrees. They did something else, too—they did some learning on the job. They learned how to work, even if it was hot, tiresome, or downright unpleasant. Fred developed an avocational ↝ interest in nature when he decided that birdsong was worth listening to and floral patterns were incredibly varied. Perhaps these patterns will one day subconsciously affect his work as an architect. Rafael learned how to listen to people, to please them, and to make them notice him. He was developing talents that would later help him become a widely respected lawyer. Every job has potential for self-education. To gain the most from a job, act in such a way that your education and your employer's needs are not in conflict.

- Compared to Fred and Rafael, Tamika carefully planned and prepared for her first job. She felt confident that just being employed and receiving a paycheck would be a great experience. She would finally be able to buy her clothes without parental approval. Throughout high school, she resisted many suggestions from her teachers that she take college entrance courses, but she never expressed her reasons for this refusal. Although she was very intelligent, her family frequently told her that they would not support her going to college—that it was "unladylike." Tamika lacked enough self-esteem and determination to seek work commensurate *ly* with her abilities. She could not conceive of attending night school classes at a nearby college—again because of her family's wishes. When her employer, recognizing her potential and sympathetic to her situation, finally insisted that she go back to school on a part-time basis, she obtained her undergraduate college degree in five years. As a young researcher, she has already published a number of outstanding papers. The lesson here is that you could be stymied more by self-concepts than by realities. The best career preparation should be realistic in terms of your abilities, not your self-doubts.

- Of these six people, Roy may seem to be the luckiest. He is his own boss. The next truth removes luck from the description. For most of the past ten years, his working days have been 12 to 15 hours long, and he has often worked seven days straight. Uncertainty and terrible living conditions could have swamped his success—except that he believed in himself and really enjoyed what he was doing. His wife is a partner and professionally competent. By providing employment and services to many others, their efforts have greatly enriched their community. Presently, they can afford to take occasional vacations, and they maintain a luxurious home. But they paid their dues in terms of delayed pleasures. If you see yourself in the future as being self-employed, take note that it takes initiative, effort, and courage. However, the rewards can be generous.

- Amelia chose work that she found to be physically demanding, though mentally boring. Since almost any occupation can be turned into a creative outlet *if* you can see the possibilities, why does Amelia feel stifled? Her choice, cosmetology, could lead to product development, marketing, consulting, and writing; it need not be limited to beauty shop work.

- Trial experiences, like Amelia's, may have been unrewarding, but she can look for guidance in one of the best possible places—the community library. Most libraries now have sections on job hunting and career selection. Some of the best books are very inexpensive; their purchase could be an excellent investment. Among the books that she could be using are the following:

  - *What Color Is Your Parachute?* Richard Nelson Bolles (2000). This highly acclaimed bestseller is available by mail from the publisher. The author is the Director of the National Career Development Project. Before you commit yourself to any career direction or contemplate getting or changing any job, read this book. It clearly describes all the practical details of obtaining a job—from interviews to resumes, from handling rejection to locating resources. Richard Bolles also publishes a bi-monthly *Newsletter about Life/Work Planning*. Information about this is included in the book.

  - *Occupational Outlook Handbook*, available from the Superintendent of Documents, Government Printing Office, Washington, D.C. 20402. Current price and availability should be checked. Most large libraries have a copy. This annual publication describes 300 occupational clusters with jobs in each cluster, including duties, requisite training and qualifications, potential earnings, and the prognosis for future employment.

  - *Encyclopedia of Career and Vocational Guidance* (1993). This two-volume resource provides information useful in identifying your abilities and talents. Again, it is likely to be found in large libraries.

- Finally, consider Christine's multiple accomplishments; they are the output of an assured, highly intelligent person. Her experiences suggest that when one occupation fails to answer one's needs, it should be augmented with another outlet, a secondary activity. No one occupation carries the guarantee of being fully satisfying. In examining career choices, think of clusters of related activities that you might enjoy pursuing as a hobby. Also think of combining interests when choosing a career. For example, interests in business, art, mathematics, and engineering could lead to selecting architecture as a career.

Whatever direction you choose, however you act, be a self-starter. Pick up your own two feet and point them somewhere. Do not depend on someone else to decide for you, to tell you what to do. Ask advice. Seek information. But make up your own mind. Did you notice the title of this chapter? Everything that you do involves risk. If you do the selecting, you can best accept the results.

James A. Breaugh reported some pertinent findings in the *Academy of Management Journal*, 24,1. He discovered that people who worked hard at uncovering job openings by using their own initiative were happier and performed better than those people who answered want ads or used various employment services. Why? Probably because their efforts gave them more accurate information about available jobs and thus made them less likely to take unsuitable work.

According to Robert G. Traxel, author of *Manager's Guide to Successful Job Hunting* (1978), what most employer's "want—and hardly ever get—is a person with a gleam in the eye and a dream in the head." Can you measure up?

Write a brief imaginary account of your ideal future employment in the blank pages following this chapter or in your personal notebook. How can you get there?

Summary

☞   Your interests and ambitions direct your occupational choices.

☞   Analyze your employment for learning opportunities.

☞   The library has excellent resources to use in career planning.

Words of Wisdom

Luck is a matter of preparation meeting opportunity.   **– Oprah Winfrey**

No race can prosper till it learns that there is as much dignity in tilling a field as in writing a poem.   **– Booker T. Washington**

The person who knows "how" will always have a job. The person who knows "why" will always be his boss.   **– Diane Ravitch**

The two important things I did learn were that you are as powerful and strong as you allow yourself to be, and that the most difficult part of any endeavor is taking the first step, making the first decision.
– Robyn Davidson

The secret of joy in work is contained in one word—excellence; to know how to do something well is to enjoy it.
– Pearl Buck

One should labor so hard in youth that everything one does subsequently is easy by comparison.
– Ashley Montagu

The work of the individual still remains the spark that moves mankind ahead even more than teamwork.
– Igor Sikorsky

Your Ideas

_____

_____

_____

_____

_____

_____

_____

_____

_____

_____

_____

_____

_____

_____

_____

_____

_____

_____

_____

_____

_____

Make no little plans: they have no magic to stir men's blood ....
Make big plans, aim high in hope and work. – **Daniel H. Burnham**

Your Ideas

Life is to be lived. If you have to support yourself, you had bloody better find some way that is going to be interesting. And you don't do that by sitting around wondering about yourself.

– Katharine Hepburn

Chapter 22

Solitude

Self-chosen solitude can be a delightful gift to yourself. You can let your mind wander into doodling space, imagining, thinking, rehearsing activities, meditating ↶, mentally concentrating upon some task intensely, and withdrawing into your inner being. No one will speak to you, interrupting your reverie ↶. No one demands your attention.

Imagine that you are a potter, an artisan ↶ who works with clay to produce three-dimensional objects such as vases, bowls, and plates. Normally you share studio space with other artists, but on this particular day, you are alone. You pick up a chunk of wedged ↶ clay, enjoying the feel of its wet pressure and its smell—reminding you of garden soil after a rainfall. Then you remember a toy that you played with in your mother's garden. Your surroundings seemingly disappear as you concentrate on the potter's wheel before you. Your whole being centers on an idea that leads you to create an abstraction of that toy in clay. When your friends see the final piece, they are surprised. You have "broken out of a mold," produced something that you had never before thought of—in a solitude intruded upon by physical sensations and memories. Did being alone enhance your creativity? Possibly, but even when no other person shared your space, you still had company—your human nature and its sociable extensions. Characteristically, people are sociable. In isolation, your thoughts over that prolonged period of time probably involved other people, other places, and other times. So you were never totally alone.

Finding Solitude

When you share living space with others, when you are almost constantly surrounded by people, the opportunities for solitude diminish. How do you find this "space?" By being inventive. Perhaps you can create opportunities by rearranging sleeping times. Turn a part of the night into day and vice versa. As a small child, you may have used sheets to create a cave for yourself under a table. Now you can seek privacy by taking a walk to some sheltered spot, finding a quiet corner in a library, or letting family know that your residence in a particular place means that you need to sometimes be alone.

Is your occasional desire to be alone selfish? In one way, yes, because it is a natural human quality to be concerned with who you are, and who you want to be. In another way, no, because this quality time with yourself may help you become a better person, more sensitive to others, with a more fully developed conscious self.

As an exercise in self-development, try the following. In your first session, begin by doing as little as possible. Simply sit or lie down somewhere quietly for at least 10-15 minutes, though up to an hour is preferable. Close your eyes and, to the extent possible, "drown out" external sounds and sensory impressions. You may set an alarm clock to end the session if you must have definite closure. If possible, use a low volume music alarm to create a soft ending. Otherwise, let your inner spirit drift until you feel a need to stop. Then, immediately record your "quiet voyage," using whatever means you prefer. Do this for succeeding voyages with the intent of discovering the merits of this process. This is a practice with an ancient lineage ᔕᕈ, a process of meditation.

Sometimes, in the magic moments of awakening from sleep, you may sense a fullness of being. You can extend this feeling by lying down quietly. Gradually, your conscious mind perks up, intrudes, and ideas start tumbling in rapid succession. These brief moments of solitude can yield exceptional and inventive answers to problems that have been a concern to you. You may wish to keep pen and paper or a recording device by your bedside to preserve these ideas while they are clear to you.

When Solitude Is Not of Your Choosing

There is another kind of solitude—a solitude that is not of your own choosing. You may occasionally feel isolated and alone because no one understands or accepts you. Perhaps you are not popular or the "choice of the crowd," possibly even rejected by people close to you, such as your friends or family. You reasonably resent this kind of solitude. It may be of brief duration ᄰ, or it may become a long-term problem. What happens as a result of this solitude will depend upon your determination to achieve your dreams, your aspirations, and your acceptance of yourself (quite correctly) as a very special person.

How To Deal with Rejection

What should you do when you feel this kind of loneliness because of rejection? Although analyzing reasons for the problem may be helpful, such attempts may be governed more by feelings than by logic. Under stress, your insight into the actions of others may be flawed. Since you do not really know the other person's reasons for rejecting you, you must guess. You may be an incorrect "guesser," and even if you correctly surmise ᄰ the reasons, what then? If you desire to change the circumstances, you must react. But how? What will you do? Anger is the least desirable reaction, because anger tends to beget ᄰ anger. It is likely that you will worsen the situation. In contrast to the heat of anger, the icy cold withdrawal into yourself may occur. You may retreat, isolating yourself from almost all human interaction. This is also a mistake, even a tragedy, because everyone belongs somewhere within the vast panoply ᄰ of humanity. All of your special qualities and talents will remain hidden and unshared if you withdraw. Here are some suggestions to help you deal with feelings of isolation:

- Realize that this is a common experience. Dr. Goleman states in his book, *Emotional Intelligence*, "... the feeling of being rejected and friendless is one most everyone goes through at some point in childhood or adolescence."

- Try to develop a larger perspective and an optimistic attitude. The actions of a few do not represent all of humanity; you can turn your attention elsewhere to find acceptance.

- Actively seek help from at least one sympathetic person (family member, teacher, doctor) whose opinions and judgment you value. Evaluate their advice carefully.

- Develop the ability to respond positively to others; take their occasional arrows and blunt them. Knowledge of human nature, known as psychology, is useful. Libraries and bookstores have numerous books on psychology.

- Make use of the calming milieu ᨒ of being outdoors. Go for a walk. Visit a park or a garden. This may be a source of inner peace and an antidote to interpersonal problems.

- Consider that perhaps the problem is not you and not others. Instead, examine whether it occurs because you are in the wrong place at the wrong time. If so, eventual changes will likely solve the problem.

- Develop proficiency in some activity that you enjoy and that is widely admired. You will probably meet people with similar interests who could become your companions and friends. As your proficiency develops, you will find that celebrity status wins friends, attracts crowds, and diminishes "aloneness."

One of the most inspiring humans who suffered incredible childhood isolation became a famous writer and counselor for the American Foundation for the Blind—Helen Keller 📖. Her disability, being blind and deaf as a result of a disease she suffered from when only 19 months old, deprived her of all normal human communication until a teacher and friend, Anne Sullivan Macy 📖, was able to breach that terrifying silence. Eventually, Helen Keller learned to speak. She graduated from Radcliffe College *cum laude* in 1904, and subsequently received honorary degrees from universities all over the world. Many of her books tell of her early isolation and later triumphs. You may realize from this brief description of her achievements that her disabilities and non-voluntary isolation had positive results both for Ms. Keller and the larger world.

An extraordinary book by Prudence Kohl, *Hole in the Garden Wall* (1998), with exquisite photographs, intensely personal essays, and poetry, contains a quote that is relevant here.

To be alone is a matter of choice,
To be lonely is a matter of circumstance.
One is a conscious decision;
The other, a cry for help.

Involuntary isolation can enhance the creative efforts of those determined to meet its challenge, even in this least joyous type of solitude. The cry for help is answered by one's own problem-solving in many instances. For example, efforts by prisoners have included mentally improving a skill, such as playing golf or the piano, by imagining its performance over and over again. Even with no paper or laptop computer available, books have been written, mathematical systems invented, poetry created, and letters to loved ones constructed—all in the mind of the person. These coping mechanisms made their confinement more bearable and less destructive to their humanity.

How can you use this information? Hopefully, you will never experience the solitude of imprisonment, abandonment, isolating illness, or physical disabilities. However, if any of these should occur to you, know that you can not only survive, but actually can creatively turn a limitation into an opportunity. You would have illustrious predecessors: Sir Thomas More 📖, Sir Walter Raleigh 📖, John Bunyan 📖, Fyodor Dostoevsky 📖, Ludwig van Beethoven 📖, Francisco Goya Y Lucientes 📖, Henri Matisse 📖, Vincent Van Gogh 📖, and Nelson Mandela 📖, among others.

During World War II, Dr. Victor Frankl was a prisoner in a Nazi concentration camp for years during which he analyzed why some prisoners were able to survive, whereas others perished. After the war, he wrote his powerful book, *Man's Search for Meaning*. In the 1980's, the journalist and political hostage Terry Anderson 📖 was able to survive the incredibly harsh circumstances of isolation by using various mental means, such as designing crossword puzzles, writing poetry, and mentally revisiting previous events. He describes his experiences in the book, *Den of Lions: Memoirs of Seven Years*. The actor Christopher Reeves 📖 became paralyzed from the neck down as a result of an accident and has had to endure a very confining isolation. His courage and determination to continue the creative use of his many talents is inspirational. Although Nelson Mandela endured the limitations and anguish of his years in prison, he has become an exceptional orator, leader, and humanitarian. Anthony Sampson has written a fascinating authorized autobiography of Mr. Mandela. You may wish to investigate these people's stories and develop some personal response such as writing a letter to them, writing a poem, or recording their kind of experience in a creative way.

Consider your life as a juggling act in which events, people, and objects tumble constantly up and down in a pattern that would be frenetic ⌒ if you could not " freeze the action" in order to see what is really happening. Your inner solitude is the camera snapshot that produces these still images which you then can examine, value, enjoy, and use to create your own tableau ⌒of reality. You must choose where to place the camera. It can be pointed at the real-world juggling act, or it can be aimed at a surrealistic ⌒ stream of images in your mind.

On Being an Introvert

What if you are a "loner," an introvert who simply enjoys and prefers solitude and sometimes requires an extensive amount of isolation? It may be natural for you to use reading, watching TV, and the computer as a replacement for the real world. Then your still camera images will be blurred, a copy of the real thing. Nevertheless, these images may be very useful creatively; the surreal oftentimes has its own particular fascination because of its dream-like quality. But when you need a clear picture of the world as it is, you have to march, wade, stride, crawl, or walk out into it.

Consider the difference in the impact of seeing pictures of a bloodied stranger versus actually bandaging a friend who is injured and moaning. There is also a major difference between reading a joke versus telling that joke to someone who is waiting for the punch line. Knowing that rap music exists and listening to it are quite dissimilar experiences. In order to develop genuine empathy for others, you must have a clear picture of contemporary culture so that you can snap realistic still shots of the daily "juggling act." You need to be where the action is—involved in face-to-face human interactions. True substitution for sociability is impossible.

Do you question whether most of your knowledge of humanity is based upon hearsay or second-hand information? Are you willing and able to directly judge and understand people? Or are you content to simply use an external norm, some assumed and unexamined standard of behavior, as a measure of what you can and will do in response to being with people? Do you realize that how you value others will influence how they value you? Have you thought about developing a balance between solitude and social mingling in your life so that they are in reasonable proportion? These are serious questions that require serious thought. If you are an introvert, such contemplation may be an enjoyable task.

On Being an Extrovert

What if you are an extrovert? If so, your camera produces floods of focused pictures because the real world attracts you, and you are extremely sociable. This personality trait may be an inborn predisposition &⁀, or it could result from imitating the habits of family members or from limited opportunities for solitude because of crowded living conditions. However, the extent of your immersion in reality can actually be a problem. Your clear pictures are from direct experience, but they need to be placed in some order that has personal meaning. You tend to avoid the contemplative solitude that is needed to examine these images in a way that creates "picture order" and significance to you. The soliloquy &⁀, "Why is this beautiful? Where can I use that? What should I keep?" is important. Why? It helps in developing your persona &⁀, in your becoming a "character," someone you would want to have as a friend.

As an extrovert, you may need to ask yourself if you are afraid to be alone. If solitude frightens you, then you should ask why. You will be with you for the rest of your life. No one else could be a better friend. Have you ever created a named playmate wholly from your imagination? This imaginary creature really exists inside you, constantly there. Your inner self is the only one fully aware of your unique and total history, capable of understanding you, able to help you laugh at yourself, often chattering in response to sensory input. This inner self really desires serious talk and meaningful conversation, at least occasionally. Why not indulge yourself sometimes, quietly and alone?

Although labels are applied as easily to both canned groceries and people, the actual content inside is more complex than indicated by a label. Probably no one could be completely introverted or extroverted. You are occasionally more one than the other, and that adds a challenge to each day and maybe even to each moment of each day. What label is most suitable for you right now?

There are two extremes in living styles that relate to solitude. One is the simple cabin-in-the-woods experience of Henry David Thoreau 📖. The other extreme is the opulent &⁀ hideaway of celebrities, where the privacy of the occupants is protected by many employees. Some examples of the latter have included the homes of William Randolph Hearst 📖, Frank Sinatra 📖, Elvis Presley 📖, and Bill Gates 📖. You may realize that, despite their extreme differences, the common similarity is the real need to be alone—at least occasionally.

Dr. Jane Piirto, in her book *Understanding Those Who Create*, includes a section on solitude. Among other ideas, she states:

> *In creative people's lives, their work is often the most important thing. Others achieve inner peace through their spirituality, through contemplations of nature, art, or music, or through exercise. All of these are usually done alone. Creative people may be solitary, but that doesn't make them neurotic or unhappy.*

Time alone apart from others may be essential for the concentration needed to write, to bring forth that which is new or invented, and to live fully. The imaginative eye can be turned inward, seeking truth internally, possibly with an aching desire to better see and serve the "madding crowd" 〰 from a perspective of isolation. It may be that the most sublime reaches of creative people occur in narrowed spaces, with limited human contacts, and in a stillness great enough to make their own heartbeats noisily obvious. Perhaps in solitude you will become more fully human.

Imagine this: the potter's wheel spins out a shape that opens your imagination. Suddenly, solitude becomes a soul-filling adventure with tickling, joyous laughter. While the universe is shrinking, you think of a special salute to Stephen Hawkins 📖, the renowned physicist who lives in a wheelchair. Then you step up to the landscape of courage and walk right through it.

Now, in solitude, record your response to the ideas of this chapter in the blank pages that follow or in your personal notebook.

☞   Solitude is a common human need.

☞   The proportion of solitude in your life is important.

☞   Your need and opportunities for solitude vary.

☞   Meditation can help you develop personally and creatively.

☞   Self-chosen solitude can enhance your creativity.

☞   It is possible to make creative use of enforced solitude.

☞   You can use various techniques to decrease the stress of social isolation.

☞   You can be solitary, creative, and happy.

Our language has wisely sensed the two sides of being alone. It has created the word "loneliness" to express the pain of being alone. And it has created the word "solitude" to express the glory of being alone.

– Paul Tillich

Talents are best nurtured in solitude; character is best formed in the stormy billows of the world.　　**– J. W. von Goethe**

Solitude is as needful to the imagination as society is wholesome for the character.

– James Russell Lowell

When we cannot bear to be alone, it means we do not properly value the only companion we have from birth to death—ourselves.

– Eda LeShan

Friendship needs no words—it is loneliness relieved of the anguish of loneliness.

– Dag Hammarskjold

The artist, however faithful to his personal vision of reality, becomes the last champion of the individual mind and sensibility against an intrusive society and an officious state. The great artist is thus a solitary figure. He has, as (Robert) Frost said "a lover's quarrel with the world."

– John F. Kennedy

Your Ideas

_____

_____

_____

_____

_____

_____

_____

_____

_____

_____

_____

_____

_____

_____

_____

_____

_____

_____

_____

_____

_____

_____

People are lonely because they build walls instead of bridges.
– J. F. Newton

Your
Ideas

_____

_____

_____

_____

_____

_____

_____

_____

_____

_____

_____

_____

_____

_____

_____

_____

_____

_____

_____

_____

To be alone is to be different. To be different is to be alone.
– Suzanne Gordon

Chapter 23

All of Your Tomorrows

All of your tomorrows begin with today. What you do today probably will have an effect on your future; however, the extent of this influence may not be obvious for a long time. Considerable wisdom is required to see the cause and effect of each day's activities. You may have a strong tendency to see the activities of *other* people and circumstances as being more influential on you. However, many times it is *your* attitude and effort that determine the outcome of any situation.

- Develop a "take charge" attitude; be in command of yourself and maintain a determination to reach your goals.
- Let your dreams and desires sweep your past uncertainties.
- Work optimistically for a future that can satisfy your best inner self.

Predicting the future is a challenging and uncertain process. At present, the future seems certain to include greater use of robots and computers. There is growing concern about the commercial use and distribution of natural resources. Changes appear certain in financial institutions, transportation systems, and social services. Bioengineering, geological exploration, computer system development, health sciences technology, and agricultural technology seem to have great career potential. However, there always is a need for people with abilities, ideas, and willingness to work hard in *any* field.

It can be tempting to make predictions, but it is sobering to realize the extent to which past predictions have failed. Two examples are especially interesting—first, the predicted near destruction of humanity by starvation in the mid-1950s, and second, the prediction of an overabundance of electrical energy by the mid-1970s. If the former had come true, the latter would certainly be true—assuming that the remnant population maintained existing power plants. Both predictions were based on what *was* currently sound knowledge at that time. The starvation concept arose in the nineteenth century as a result of examining converging ᏻ graphs of rising population and diminishing sources of fixed nitrogen needed for plant growth and food stores. It overlooked the possibility of technological invention, however, which did occur. The chemical fixation of nitrogen by the Haber 📖 process in the early twentieth century permitted the manufacture of chemical fertilizers and thus averted the starvation crisis. Excess power production was an extrapolation ᏻ based on the initial stages of nuclear power plant design. It was thought that electric power would become so plentiful and cheap that metering for household use would be unnecessary. This prediction failed for many reasons, including an unrealistic assessment of total production costs.

Preparing for a Less Than Certain Future

What can you do to prepare for a less-than-certain tomorrow? The following suggestions can help. You may recognize a number of them because of their inclusion in previous chapters.

- Make an effort to learn as much as possible about people, their nature, and their needs. Take a good psychology course, educate yourself by using library facilities, and become a careful observer. Study yourself—but beware of becoming *too* self-concerned.

- Remember that any change tends to disturb more than the immediate item or circumstance. Try to evaluate the "ripple effect."

- When something goes wrong or needs changing, seek advice from at least one impartial source (it could be a person or a book) *and* from someone who knows you and cares about you. Use the advice when possible.

- Begin accumulating a personal money fund—it will be a good cushion in the event of a needed career change or any other upset. Treat money with respect, not avarice &. Be aware of the social implications of your expenditures. Your spending becomes a statement of support for a product, an event, or anything else. Somehow, somewhere, money has a human value in goods produced or work expended. Therefore, in spending money you are using an exchange of human effort.

- Read *local* newspapers, and, if possible, at least one other national paper—such as the *New York Times*, the *Christian Science Monitor*, or the *Washington Post*.

- Read at least one foreign journal or newspaper on a regular basis. Explore the Internet, and the many foreign publications available on-line. Check the public library for possibilities. By comparison with indigenous & papers and magazines, the differences in points of view and values may be useful in assessing future political changes.

- Maintain membership in at least one group active in community affairs. This gives you a way to scan the horizon for changes within your immediate area.

- On a regular basis (use your personal calendar), evaluate your present circumstances as they relate to your long-range goals. Use creative thinking to figure out possible changes. Do this when you are in a good mood.

- Live each day as fully and as honorably as you can—perhaps as though each day might be your last one.
- Read—regularly, widely, and carefully.
- Evaluate the importance or value of anything by using a time perspective. Ask yourself, "How important will this be in a week, a month, a year ...?"
- Attend conferences and workshops. Take courses. Write. Create. Publish. Speak. Share your ideas. Explore the Internet.
- Regularly and rigorously examine your code of ethics and your current working and living circumstances. Do they agree? If not, what should you do?
- Maintain a social life. Beware of isolation.
- Attend cultural events as often as possible. Remember that the art world, for example, not only mirrors the present—it often gives a glimpse of the future.
- Become active politically. Political processes shape the future. Volunteer work is an excellent way to gather insights.
- Read: *The Tyranny of Survival and Other Pathologies of Civilized Life* by Daniel Callahan (1973); *Surviving the Future* by Arnold Toynbee (1971); *Global Trends 2005: An Owner's Manual for the Next Decade* by Michael J. Mazarr (1999); *State of the World 2000* by Worldwatch Institute (2000), and similar books.
- If change suddenly swamps you, reach for a "bail-out bucket." What should the bucket contain? A large helping of confidence. You are "very okay." Whatever happens, know that you *will* manage.

Understanding Allegorical Symbolism

One of the primary purposes of this book is to help you respond creatively to opportunities. This last exercise involves an opportunity to decode symbols in an allegory. Understanding symbolism is the first step to interpreting this allegory. Symbolism, when used in literary contexts, involves the use of specific words and phrases to represent thoughts, ideas, or objects. But, as Merlin Donald points out in his book, *Origins of the Modern Mind: Three Stages in the Evolution of Culture and Cognition*, "… to understand or use a symbol appropriately in context you must first understand what it represents, and this referential understanding is inherently non-symbolic." Just knowing that symbols exist does little to enhance creative efforts. It is the invention of symbols and the subsequent investigation of meaning that is associated with creative acts. For example, a dictionary is a symbolic system, but it does not account for the sequencing of these symbols in creative writing. Nor does it adequately explain the frequent ambiguity ᚷ in word usage. Otherwise, the best writing of any kind—novel, poem, play, scientific—could be considered to be merely a rearranged dictionary. The sense of these ideas will become apparent if you ever attempt to use a foreign language dictionary to engage in conversation with someone natively fluent in that language. Results can range from hazardous to hilarious.

In decoding allegories, you seek pathways of understanding between the writing and your imagination. Developing these relationships provides a useful fusion of ideas from many sources.

Thought and language are twinned aspects of mental acuity ᚷ—each helping in the extension and enrichment of the other. New ideas extend language in the interpretive sense and sometimes literally, as with the many new words created with the evolution of computer use. Where thought crosses the boundaries of known material representation, symbolism is essential to both understanding and evaluating those thoughts. For example, thinking about mythical creatures such as Pegasus 📖 requires the use of symbols for representation, since Pegasus does not exist. Such symbolic use also is a factor when you consider intangibles such as beliefs and feelings in allegorical writing. Concepts related to human existence frequently are loaded with variable meaning, encoded in culturally accepted symbols.

Excavating meaning from writing or other symbolic usage literally converts concepts to your authorship or ownership. Of course, reasonably, you tend to follow the guiding parameters ∽ of the original concepts. What you add is personal involvement— seasoning to a mental broth. To illustrate this process, the allegory *The Hourglass* and some possible imaginative seasonings (or decodings) follow.

The Hourglass

A piece of earth, a sand grain of quartz lifted skyward and swirled a great distance, enters the complex town of Eversame one morning. It bounces against a long fence; then it drops into a groove in a toy chest. The chest, which is painted red and blue, is lodged in a clump of wild asparagus.

The next spring, a woman searching for food mutters, "that careless child." As she rubs the toy box clean, the sand grain falls and clings to her sock. At home, in the wash water from her clothes, the sand grain sinks into the water table. There, the tiny particle spends years before being carried to a stream edge.

On one clouded fall day, the same sand grain sticks to the side of the yellow boot of an old man. While he patiently sits on the stream bank fishing, he dreams— remembering childhood friends and their games with the contents of a red and blue toy chest. Walking back to the highway, the sand grain drops from his boot. On the next windy day the grain is conveyed by a car tire to an unknown destination.

This allegory, *The Hourglass*, is a symbolic narrative. Its most interesting aspect is not the story line—it is the meaning that you can assign to it. Your sense of the code will be affected by your experiences, knowledge, feelings, and beliefs—every aspect of your being. This decoding process varies from person to person, and there are no absolutely right or wrong answers. At another time, even your interpretation may change.

As a suggestion, read the entire story and set it aside for a few days. At a second reading, imagine how you could connect the words to an overall meaning or theme. Record your ideas on paper or computer. Test your theme by assigning meaning to phrases or words in the first few sentences. For *The Hourglass*, time, change, ideas, ecology, and human interaction all seem to be possible themes. If a distinctive phrase or word is repeated throughout, give it a specific identity. Making everything fit within your selected theme is a challenge—a kind of mental game.

One possible interpretation, using the theme of ideas, follows (phrases and terms from the allegory are italicized):

One Possible Interpretation

A piece of earth, a sand grain of quartz—an idea—*lifted skyward and swirled a great distance*—arrives from outside (foreign)—*enters the complex town of Eversame one morning*—the town, as suggested by its title, has a social structure not receptive to change and strange ideas. *It bounces against a long fence*—a barrier to ideas or a boundary that both includes and excludes ideas—*then it drops into a groove in a toy chest. The chest, which is painted red and blue, is lodged in a clump of wild asparagus*—reception of a new idea associated with youth (toy chest) as well as "wild" food for thought (asparagus).

The next spring, a woman searching for food mutters, "thJat careless child"—concern that the toy box was lost or abandoned; an act against social standards? Or perhaps it is an indication of the limits of play. *As she rubs the toy box clean, the sand grain falls and clings to her sock*—the sand grain, the idea, attaches to the covering of her feet, the part most capable of physically moving self in a new direction. *At home, in the wash water from her clothes*—inability, chosen or accidental, to keep the new concept—*the sand grain sinks into the water table*—ideas not accepted, worked with, or neglected are stored somewhere merely needing discovery. *There, the tiny particle*—initially ideas may seem small, unimportant—*spends years*—some ideas, especially those of social change, require a long time prior to acceptance, especially in places like Eversame—*before being carried to a stream edge*—an active proponent ᴇᴧ of an idea is needed to release it into a current stream of thought.

On *one clouded fall day*—for most people, less than ideal conditions exist for some idea transfers—*the same sand grain sticks to the side of the yellow boot*—ideas as mere "footnotes" to living—*of an old man*—now have three persons mentioned and more implied in the existence of a town. If they are archetypal ᴇᴧ, what do they represent in a status quo Eversame place? Woman: food supplier, child care, cleaning; Child: play, learning; Man: employed (yellow boots), food supplier, recreation. Could ideas change these roles for some people or some times? *While he patiently sits on the stream bank fishing*—anyone of any age can go fishing for ideas—*he dreams—remembering*—more active effort needed to hold onto ideas—*childhood friends and their games with the contents of a red and blue toy chest*—primary colors (including yellow boots) represent ideas held in primary esteem. *Walking back to the highway, the sand grain drops from his boot*—leaving that idea behind. *On the next windy day the grain is conveyed by a car tire to an unknown destination*—an optimistic ending; the unrecognized idea still exists, waiting for discovery.

Could this allegory be decoded in a better way, perhaps using a dual theme of time and ideas? Are ideas time-dependent in all their aspects from realization to acceptance? Numerous examples of this dependency exist throughout history. For example, the discovery of the pattern of blood circulation normally is attributed to the British anatomist William Harvey 📖. Yet Hildegard of Bingen 📖 (born 1098) described the same ideas in a treatise ᴇᴧ 500 years earlier than Harvey. She also noted the link between diabetes and sugar, as well as the probable transmission of signals from the brain to the body along the nerves. These ideas were premature with respect to the social and cultural framework of her lifetime—thus they were rendered useless to society and she gained no recognition for her ideas. In a sense, her ideas rolled down the highway of time waiting for recognition.

What is next? Write some responses to this decoding in the work pages at the end of this chapter. You could make your own analysis of *The Hourglass*, satisfying your viewpoints. *The Next Sunrise*, which follows, is another allegory for your interpretation. You might try writing your own allegory or perhaps finding another allegory to interpret. Many were written during Greek and Roman times and can be found in classical literature.

The Next Sunrise

Imagine that you are walking in a vast meadow with the morning song of birds orchestrating pleasure. Distantly, you perceive what appears to be a huge, white rock tilted against a blue horizon. As you head toward it, the sky darkens, a tumble of rain blurs the distance, and you slog onward. There is no shelter.

When the hot sun dries you, the rock reappears—no longer white, and also smaller in size. You must have walked away from it during the storm. You long to talk to someone, but there is no one in sight.

Should you continue? Is it that important? You proceed toward the rock. A small toad hops away from you, reminding you to be careful of your steps. A tiny piece of foil catches your eye. You shape it gently and prop it on top of a daisy.

Now the rock begins to have a shape like a tablet, and its long shadow almost touches you. The sun sets, and the colors suffuse the long grass blades. An image of green daggers troubles you.

You reach the rock just in time to see faint lettering chipped in it—your name shocks you for a moment. Then you realize that everyone has the same name—Human. With a sense of satisfaction, you lean against it for a comfortable sleep.

The next sunrise glints its beam from the foil to a sleepy toad.

You may also enjoy decoding various artworks of known allegorical origin. For example, Thomas Cole's paintings, "The Voyage of Life," at the National Gallery of Art in Washington, D.C. symbolically represents the four stages of life. Many prints from the eighteenth and nineteenth centuries likewise carry allegorical significance. Certain plays, many poems, and some musical compositions have been created with concealed meaning. Your sensitivity to hidden ideas and your interest in decoding that which is mysterious can be a pleasing and useful adventure.

The future is yours—dotted, striped, green, tough, rocky, tender, flat, tumultuous—all yours!

Words
of
Wisdom

The way I see it, if you want a rainbow, you gotta put up with the rain.
– Dolly Parton

I like living. I have sometimes been wildly, despairingly, acutely miserable, racked with sorrow, but through it all I still know quite certainly that just to be alive is a grand thing.
– Agatha Christie

I began to have an idea of my life, not as the slow shaping of achievement to fit my pre-conceived purposes, but as the gradual discovery and growth of a purpose which I did not know.
– Joanna Field

Talent is the gift plus the passion—a desire to succeed so intense that no force on earth can stop it.
– Neil Simon

My interest is in the future—because I'm going to spend the rest of my life there.
– Charles F. Kettering

Life, for all its agonies of despair and loss and guilt, is exciting and beautiful, amusing and artful and endearing, full of liking and love, at times a poem and a high adventure, at times noble and at times very gay; and whatever (if anything) is to come after it— we shall not have this life again.
– Rose Macaulay

Your Ideas

_____

_____

_____

_____

_____

_____

_____

_____

_____

_____

_____

_____

_____

_____

_____

_____

_____

_____

_____

_____

_____

_____

_____

_____

Who in the world am I? Ah, that's the great puzzle. **– Lewis Carroll**

Your Ideas

_____

_____

_____

_____

_____

_____

_____

_____

_____

_____

_____

_____

_____

_____

_____

_____

_____

_____

_____

The best way to make your dreams come true is to wake up.
– J. M. Power

All-Time Great Books

Aeschylus: *Oresteia; Prometheus Bound*

Aristophanes: *The Frogs; Plutus; Lysistrata; The Clouds*

Aristotle: *The Poetics; Ethics; The Art of Poetry*

Augustine: *Confessions*

Aurelius: *Meditations*

The Bible: *Genesis; Amos; Job; Matthew; John; Romans*

Cervantes: *Don Quixote*

Dante: *Inferno*

Dostoyevsky: *Crime and Punishment*

Euripides: *Electra; Iphigenia in Taurus; Hippolytus; Medea; The Bacchae*

Fielding: *Tom Jones*

Goethe: *Faust, Part 1 and 2*

Herodotus: *The Persian Wars*

Homer: *Iliad; Odyssey*

Lucretius: *On the Nature of Things*

Machiavelli: *The Prince*

Milton: *Paradise Lost*

Moliere: *Tartuffe; The Misanthrope; The Physician in Spite of Himself; School for Wives*

Montaigne: *Essays*

Plato: *Ion; Apology; Republic; Phaedo; Symposium*

Rabelais: *Gargantua and Pantagruel*

Rousseau: *Confessions*

Shakespeare: *Henry IV, Parts 1 and 2; King Lear; Anthony and Cleopatra; The Tempest*

Sophocles: *Oedipus the King; Antigone; Ajax; Philoctetes*

Spinoza: *Ethics*

Swift: *Gulliver's Travels*

Thucydides: *The History of the Peloponnesian War*

Virgil: *Aeneid*

Voltaire: *Candide*

References in Chapters

Adizes, I. (1992). *Mastering change: The power of mutual trust and respect in personal life, family life, business, and society.* Santa Monica, CA: Adizes Institute Publications. (ISBN 0-937120-04-9)

Anderson, T. A. (1993). *Den of lions: Memoirs of seven years.* New York: Crown Publishers. (ISBN 0-517-59301-7)

Austin, L. (2000). *What's holding you back: 8 critical choices for women's success.* New York: Basic Books. (ISBN 0-465-03262-1)

Berg, H. S. & Conyers, M. (1998). *Speed reading: The easy way.* New York: Barron's Publications. (ISBN 0-8120-9852-8)

Bolles, R. N. (1999). *The 2000 What color is your parachute?* Berkley, CA: Ten Speed Press. (ISBN 0-89815-931-8)

Breaugh, J. A. (1981). Relationships between recruiting sources and employee performance, absenteeism and work attitude. *Academy of Management Journal, 24 (1),* 142-147.

Brown, B. B. (1974). *New mind, new body, bio-feedback: New directions for the mind.* New York: Harper & Row. (ISBN 0-06010-159-6)

Callahan, D. (1985). *The tyranny of survival and other pathologies of civilized life*. Lanham, MD: University Press of America. (ISBN 0-8191-4636-6)

Carson, R. (1987). *Silent spring (25th Anniversary issue)*. Boston: Houghton Mifflin Co. (ISBN 0-3965-53909)

Cook, H. & Davitz, J. (1975). *60 seconds to mind expansion*. New York: Random House. (ISBN 0-3944-9797-X)

Cosgrove, H. (Ed.). (1997). *Encyclopedia of career and vocational guidance, 10th ed.* Chicago: Ferguson Publishing Co. (ISBN 0-89434-170-7)

Covey, S. R. (1990). *The seven habits of highly effective people*. New York: Simon & Schuster. (ISBN 0-671-70863-5)

Donald, M. (1991). *Origins of the modern mind: Three stages in the evolution of culture and cognition*. Cambridge, MA: Harvard University Press. (ISBN 0-674-644483-2)

Duke, P. &Hochman, G. (1993). *A brilliant madness, living with manic depression illness*. New York: Bantam Books. (ISBN 0-553-56072-7)

Dyer, W. (1990). *The sky's the limit*. Seattle, WA: McGraw Mountain, Inc. (ISBN 0-671-72565-3)

Eliot, T. S. (1955). *The wasteland and other poems*. San Diego, CA: Harvest Books. (ISBN 0-15-694877-X)

Epstein, J. (1989). *Ambition, the secret passion*. Chicago: Elephant Paperbacks. (ISBN 0-929587-18-9)

Freese, A. S. (1973). *Headaches, the kinds and cures*. New York: Doubleday. (ISBN 0-3850-3966-2)

Gephart, R. & Wessel, M. (1999). *An even better place: America in the 21st century*. New York: Public Affairs. (ISBN 1-891620-16-9)

Giano, J. (1985). *The man who planted trees*. White River Junction, VA: Chelsea Green Publishing Co. (ISBN 0-930031-06-7)

Girard, J. (1986). *How to sell anything to anybody*. New York: Warner Books. (ISBN 0-446-38532-8)

Goldman, D. R. FACP (Editor-in-chief). (1999). *American College of Physician's complete home medical guide*. New York: DK Publishing, Inc. (ISBN 0-7894-44127)

Goleman, D. (1995). *Emotional intelligence*. New York: Bantam Books. (ISBN 0-553-09503-X)

Herriot, J. (1974). *All things bright and beautiful*. New York: St. Martin's Press. (ISBN 0-312-02030-9)

Kapleau, P. (1989). *The three pillars of Zen*. Two Harbors, MN: Anchor Books. (ISBN 0-3852-6093-8)

Keller, H. A. (1957). *The open door*. Garden City, NY: Doubleday. (LC No. 57-013019)

Keller, H. A. (1903). *The story of my life*. New York: Doubleday. (ISBN 0-5532-1387-3)

Kennedy, J. F. (1994). *Profiles in courage*. Catchogue, NY: Buccaneer Books. (ISBN 1-5684-9553-6)

Kohl, P. (1988). *Hole in the garden wall*. Beachwood, Ohio: Cyrano Guildmaster Publishing. (ISBN 0-945299-00-1)

Liebman, J. L. (1994). *Peace of mind*. Secaucus, NJ: Carol Publishing Group. (ISBN 0-8065-1496-5)

Lindbergh, A. M. (1991). *Gift from the sea*. New York: Random House. (ISBN 0-679-7341-1)

Marsh, P. (1988). *Eye to eye: How people interact*. Toppsfield, MA: Salem House Publishers. (ISBN 0-88162-371-7)

Mazarr, M. J. (1999). *Global trends 2005: An owner's manual for the next decade*. New York: St. Martin's Press. (ISBN 0-312-21899-0)

McGraw, P. C. (1999). *Life strategies: Doing what works, doing what matters*. New York: Hyperion. (ISBN 0-7868-6548-2)

Molloy, J. T. (1996). *The new woman's dress for success*. New York: Warner Books, Inc. (ISBN 0-446-67223-8)

Molloy, J. T. (1988). *John T. Molloy's new dress for success.* New York: Warner Books, Inc. (ISBN 0-446-38552-2)

Molloy, J. T. (1983). *Molloy's live for success.* New York: Bantam Books. (ISBN 0-553-23515-X)

Occupational Outlook Handbook (annual publication). Washington, DC 20402: Superintendent of Documents, Government Printing Office.

Piirto, J. (1998). *Understanding those who create, 2ⁿᵈ ed.* Scottsdale, AZ: Gifted Psychology Press, Inc. (ISBN 0-910707-27-8)

Pitino, R. & Reynolds, B. L. (1997). *Success is a choice: Ten steps to overachieving in business and life.* New York: Broadway Books. (ISBN 0-553-06668-4)

Rand, A. (1964). *The virtue of selfishness.* New York: NAL – Dutton. (ISBN 0-451-15699-4)

Rozakis, L. E. (1999). *The complete idiot's guide to public speaking, 2ⁿᵈ ed.* New York: Alpha Books. (ISBN 0-02-863383-0)

Sampson, A. (1999). *Mandela: The authorized biography.* New York: Alfred A. Knopf. (ISBN 0-375-40019-2)

Scheele, A. M. (1996). *Skills for success: A guide to the top for men and women.* New York: Ballantine. (ISBN 0-345-41044-0)

Simeons, A. T. (1961). *Man's presumptuous brain: An evolutionary interpretation.* New York: NAL- Dutton. (ISBN 0-5254-7109-X)

Thomas, P. G. (1979). *Psychofeedback.* Paramus, NJ: Prentice Hall. (ISBN 0-1373-2263-1)

Time-Life Books Editors (1994). *Emotions: Journey through the mind and body.* Alexander, VA: Time-Life Books. (ISBN 0-7835-106-08)

Toynbee, A. (1971). *Surviving the future.* New York: Oxford University Press. (ISBN 0-1921-5252-1)

Tramel, M. E. & Reynolds, H. (1981). *Executive leadership: How to get it and make it work.* New York: Prentice Hall. (ISBN 0-1329-4124-4)

Traxel, R. G. (1978). *Manager's guide to successful job hunting.* New York: McGraw Hill. (ISBN 0-0706-5096-9)

Vital Speeches of the Day (bi-monthly). Mt. Pleasant, SC: City News Publishing Co.

Woolf, V. (1990). *Mrs. Dalloway.* San Diego, CA: Harvest Books. (ISBN 0-15-662870-8)

WorldWatch Institute (2000). *State of the world 2000.* New York: W.W. Norton and Company, Inc. (ISBN 0-393-31998-9)

Recommended Readings

Agosin, M. (Ed.), Giachetti, M. (Translator) (1993). *A Gabriela mistral reader.* Fredonia, NY: White Pine Press. (ISBN 1-877727-18-0)

Ayan, J. (1997). *Aha! 10 ways to free your creative spirit and find your great ideas.* New York: Crown Trade Paperbacks. (ISBN 0-517-88400-3)

Baskin, Y. (1997). *The work of nature: How the diversity of life sustains us.* Washington, DC: Island Press. (ISBN 1-55963-519-3)

Bernstein, P. L. (1996). *Against the gods: The remarkable story of risk.* New York: John Wiley & Sons, Inc. (ISBN 0-471-12104-5)

Bohle, B. (1986). *The home book of American quotations.* New York: Gramercy Publishing Co. (ISBN 0-517-60356-X)

Bronowski, J. (1973). *The ascent of man.* Boston/Toronto: Little, Brown and Co. (ISBN 0-316-10930-4)

Coleman, A. M. (1999). *What is psychology? 3rd ed.* London: Routledge. (ISBN 0-415-16901-1)

Dana, D. (1961). *Selected poems of Gabriela Mistral.* Baltimore, MD: Johns Hopkins University Press. (ISBN 0-8010-1256-9)

Dillard, A. (1990). *The writing life.* New York: Harper Perennial. (ISBN 0-06-016156-6)

Doerger, F. G. (1997). *Welcome to the real working world: What every employee must know to succeed.* Santa Monica, CA: General Publishing Group. (ISBN 1-57544-052-0)

Einstein, A. (1985). *Ideas and opinions.* New York: Crown Publishers. (ISBN 0-5175-5601-4)

Einstein, A. (1949). *The world as I see it.* New York: Philosophical Library (ISBN 0-8065-0711-X).

Eiseley, L. (1978). *The star thrower.* London: Wildwood House, Ltd. (ISBN 0-7045-3017-1)

Epstein, J. (Ed.). (1997). *The Norton book of personal essays.* New York: Norton & Company, Inc. (ISBN 0-393-03654-5)

Exley, H. (Ed.). (1993). *The best of women's quotations.* New York: Exley (ISBN 1-85015-308-6)

Fieve, R. R. (1997). *Moodswing, 2nd ed.* New York: Bantam. (ISBN 0-553-27983-1)

Foster, H. W., Jr. (1997). *Make a difference.* New York: Scribner. (ISBN 0-684-82685-2)

Fukuyama, F. (1992). *The end of history and the last man.* NY: Free Press (ISBN 0-02-910975-2).

Gamez, G. (1996). *Creativity: How to catch lightning in a bottle.* Los Angeles: Peak Publications. (ISBN 0-9650590-3-0)

Garner, A. (1991). *Conversationally speaking: Tested new ways to increase your personal and social effectiveness.* Los Angeles: Lowell House; Contemporary Books. (ISBN 0-929923-72-3)

Gell-Mann, M. (1995). *The quark and the jaguar. Adventures in the simple and the complex.* New York: W.H. Freeman and Co. (ISBN 0-7167-2725-0)

Gould, S. J. (1997). *Questioning the millennium: A rationalist's guide to a precisely arbitrary countdown.* New York: Harmony Books. (ISBN 0-609-60076-1)

Gould, S. J. (1996). *Full house: The spread of excellence from Plato to Darwin.* New York: Harmony Books. (ISBN 0-609-80140-6)

Griffin, J. (1994). *How to say it best: Choice words, phrases, & model speeches for every occasion.* New York: Prentice Hall. (ISBN 0-13-435322-6)

Hawking, S. W. (1996). *The nature of space and time.* Princeton, NJ: Princeton University Press. (ISBN 0-6910-3791-4)

Hawking, S. W. (1988). *A brief history of time: From the big bang to black holes.* New York: Bantam Books. (ISBN 0-5530-5243-8)

Haynes, M. E. (1998). *Effective meeting skills: A practical guide for more productive meetings.* Los Altos, CA: Crisp Publications, Inc. (ISBN 0-931961-33-5)

Hirsch, E. D. (1987). *Cultural literacy: What every American needs to know.* Boston: Houghton Mifflin Co. (ISBN 0-395-43095-X).

Hoff, R. (1992). *I can see you naked.* Kansas City, MO: Andrews & McMeel. (ISBN 0-8362-8000-8)

Huang, C. A. & Lynch, J. (1995). Mentoring: *The Tao of giving and receiving wisdom.* New York: HarperCollins. (ISBN 0-06-251251-X)

Kent, P. (1996). *The complete idiot's guide to the Internet.* Indianapolis: Que Corporation. (ISBN 0-7897-0862-0)

Kitwood, T. (1990). *Concern for others: A new psychology of conscience and morality.* New York: Routledge. (ISBN 0-415-04377-8)

Kottler, J. (1990). *Private moments, secret selves.* Los Angeles: Jeremy P. Tarcher, Inc. (ISBN 0-87477-493-4)

Luoma, J. R. (1999). *The hidden forest: The biography of an ecosystem.* New York: Henry Holt & Co. (ISBN 0-8050-1491-8)

Madigan, C. O. & Elwood, A. (1983). *Brainstorms & thunderbolts: How creative genius works.* New York: MacMillan Publishing Company. (ISBN 0-02-579160-5)

May, R. (1983). *The discovery of being: Writings in existential psychology.* New York: W. W. Norton & Co. (ISBN 0-393-01790-7)

McGrath, C. (Ed.). (1998). *A hundred years of authors, ideas and literature from the New York Times.* New York: Times Books. (ISBN 0-8129-2965-9)

Morse, J. D. (1979). *Old master paintings in North America.* New York: Abbeville Press. (ISBN 0-89659-050-X)

Mueller, L., & Reynolds, J. D. (1990). *Creative writing: Forms and techniques.* Lincolnwood, ILL: National Textbook Co. (ISBN 0-8442-5365-0)

Mullis, K. (1998). *Dancing naked in the mind field.* NewYork: Pantheon Books. (ISNB 0-679-44255-3)

Parini, J. (1999). *Robert Frost: A life.* New York: Henry Holt & Co. (ISBN 0-8050-3181-2)

Peacock, M. (1998). *How to read a poem and start a poetry circle.* New York: Riverhead Books. (ISBN 1-57322-128-7)

Plotnik, A. (1996). *The elements of expression.* New York: Henry Holt and Co.. (ISBN 0-8050-3773-X)

Post, E. L. (1990). *Emily Post on invitations and letters.* New York: Harper & Row Publishers. (ISBN 0-06-081037-8)

Post, E. L., & Coles, J. M. (1986). *Emily Post talks with teens about manners and etiquette.* New York: Harper & Row Publishers. (ISBN 0-06-181685-X)

Random House (1996). *Random House power vocabulary builder.* New York: Random House. (ISBN 0-345-405455)

Redway, K. (1997). *How to be a rapid reader: 6 steps to increased speed and concentration.* Lincolnwood, IL: National Textbook Company. (ISBN 0-8442-5174-7)

Reilly, J. (1992). *Mentorship: The essential guide for schools and business.* Scottsdale, AZ: Gifted Psychology Press, Inc. (ISBN 0-910707-18-9)

Rozakis, L. E. (1997). *The complete idiot's guide to creative writing.* New York: Alpha Books. (ISBN 0-02-861734-7)

Sarton, M. (1973). *Journal of a solitude.* New York: Norton & Co. (ISBN 0-393-30928-2)

Savant, M. V. & Fleischer, L. (1990). *Brain building in just 12 weeks.* New York: Bantam Books. (ISBN 0-553-35348-9)

Scheibe, K.E. (2000). *The drama of everyday life.* Boston: Harvard University Press. (ISBN 0-674-00231-8)

Seldes, G. (1985). *The great thoughts.* New York: Ballantine Books. (ISBN 0-345-2988-X)

Sheehy, E. P. (Ed.). (1986). *Guide to reference books, 10th ed.* Chicago & London: American Library Association. (ISBN 0-8389-0390-8)

Sherman, R. & Seldon, P. (1997). *The complete idiot's guide to classical music.* New York: Alpha Books. (ISBN 0-02-861634-0)

Siepmann, K. B. (Ed.). (1987). *Benet's reader's encyclopedia, 3rd ed.* New York: Harper & Row Publishers. (ISBN 0-06-181088-6)

Siever, L. J. (1997). *The new view of self: How genes and neuro-transmitters shape your mind, your personality, and your health.* New York: Macmillan. (ISBN 0-02-861544-1)

Simpson, J. B. (1988). *Simpson's contemporary quotations.* Boston: Houghton Mifflin Co. (ISBN 0-395-43085-2)

Sinatra, S. T. (1997). *Optimum health: A natural lifesaving pre-scription for your body and mind.* New York: Bantam Books. (ISBN 0-553-10613-9)

Smith, H. W. (1994). *The 10 natural laws of successful time and life management: Proven strategies for increased productivity and inner peace.* New York: Warner Books, Inc. (ISBN 0-446-51741-0)

Storr, A. (1988). *Solitude: A return to the self.* New York: Ballantine Books. (ISBN 0-345-35847-3)

Szymborska, W. (1998). *Poems: New and collected 1957-1997.* New York: Harcourt Brace & Co. (ISBN 0-15-100353-X)

Tate, J. (1991). *Selected poems.* Hanover & London: University Press of New England. (ISBN 0-8195-2190-6)

Trilling, L. & Weiseltier, L. (Eds.). (2000). *The moral obligation to be intelligent: Selected essays.* New York: Farrar, Straus & Giroux. (ISBN 0-374-25794-9)

Tucker, T. (1995). *Brainstorm!: The stories of twenty American kid inventors.* New York: Farrar, Straus & Giroux. (ISBN 0-374-30944-2)

Walters, L. (1993). *Secrets of a successful speaker: How you can motivate, captivate & persuade.* New York: McGraw-Hill, Inc. (ISBN 0-07-068034-5)

Warren, R. P. (1996). *Sixty years of American poetry: Celebrating the anniversary of the Academy of American Poets.* New York: Harry N. Abrams. (ISBN 0-8109-4464-2)

Wechsler, H. J. (1967). *Great prints et printmakers.* New York: Harry N. Abrams, Inc. (LC No. 67-12686)

Index of Names

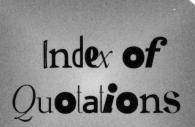

Index of Quotations

Epilogue

For You

Oh try – let your voice come
Lilting with full sounds for
Metal gilting any dark marks
On the pure golden larking
That must cover the dust of living.

Oh cry – with a song that
Slipping tantalizes the air
By ripping at the stillness
In words and rhythms
To remove the rust of living.

Oh sigh – a breath let loose
Aching any answer with
Love and caring that will
Augur and argue meaning
Central to the crust of living.

Oh fly – gather cirrus and skybolts
Flinging energy with focus
Enough kindling of desires
To challenge your faculties
And heart touch the thrust of living.

With love,
BJE

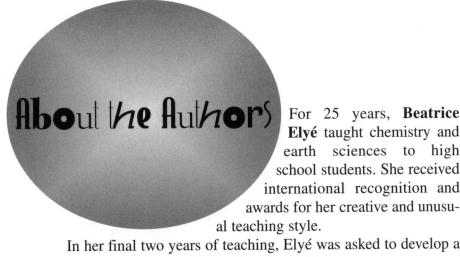

About the Authors

For 25 years, **Beatrice Elyé** taught chemistry and earth sciences to high school students. She received international recognition and awards for her creative and unusual teaching style.

In her final two years of teaching, Elyé was asked to develop a program for talented and gifted students. Her purpose was to provide information to capable students to encourage them to make better use of their abilities, as well as see the joyousness of doing so. Her program had a positive effect on the participants, who became known as *The Monday Box Group*. She wrote *JumpStart: Ideas to Move Your Mind* so that she could share her unique approach with others.

Lifelong avocations of Elyé include growing rare perennials from seed, the restoration of art, and collecting Chinese porcelains. Elyé's original garden design won the National Golden Trowel award from *Garden Design* Magazine.

Catherine Southwick is a graduate of the State University of New York at Buffalo with a Bachelor's Degree in Environmental Design. She has an additional year of Art Education course work with Buffalo State College.

Her background includes working with and teaching inner city youth, and she is employed as a mentor at Erie Community College in Buffalo, New York.

She is currently pursuing her Master's Degree in Education.